SPITFIRE
IN COMBAT

To Darling Ben -
Christmas 2004
with Bear Hugs
and Love Always
— Mumsie Mooo x
x x x x x x

SPITFIRE
IN COMBAT

A L F R E D   P R I C E

SUTTON PUBLISHING

First published in the United Kingdom in 2003 by
Sutton Publishing Limited · Phoenix Mill
Thrupp · Stroud · Gloucestershire · GL5 2BU

British Library Cataloguing in Publication Data
A catalogue record for this book is available from the British Library.

ISBN 0-7509-3160-4

Typeset in 10/13pt Sabon.
Typesetting and origination by
Sutton Publishing Limited.
Printed and bound in England by
J.H. Haynes & Co. Ltd, Sparkford.

CONTENTS

INTRODUCTION

Few would argue with the proposition that the Supermarine Spitfire was one of the most successful fighter designs ever, perhaps *the* most successful. It remained unsurpassed from the biplane era to the beginning of the jet age, a period that included the Second World War.

During that conflict nobody attempted to pull so much out of a single combat aircraft design as the Supermarine Company did with the Spitfire. And the Royal Air Force would not have needed it, had it not been forced to by the demands of war. At that time it took about three years to progress a new fighter from the drawing board into service, whereas an in-service fighter could be fitted with a more powerful engine or other modifications and brought into service within a few months. So the Spitfire had to bridge the gap until the newer fighter types were ready for service. By dint of a huge amount of improvisation, it succeeded in keeping abreast of its competitors almost to the end of the Second World War.

The Spitfire remained in production for more than twelve years. Compared with the prototype, the Mark 24 had an engine that developed twice as much power, its maximum take-off weight was more than doubled, its maximum rate of climb was nearly twice as great, it was one quarter faster and its fire power was five times greater.

In this book I have described aspects of the Spitfire story that I feel will interest both the enthusiasts on this subject and those making a study of it for the first time. The initial chapter, 'First of the Few', uses first person accounts and recently discovered archive material to shed new light on the testing of the prototype Spitfire K5054. Chapter 2, 'Spitfire into Service', recounts the various changes needed to make the Spitfire into a fully effective fighting machine. Chapter 3, 'The Speed Spitfire', describes Britain's unsuccessful attempt to prepare a much-modified Spitfire for an assault on the World Landplane Speed Record. Chapters 4 and 5 cover Fighter Command's Spitfire Order of Battle on 14 September 1940, and the part Spitfires played in the crucial air actions on 15 September 1940 which we now commemorate as 'Battle of Britain Day'. Chapter 6, 'Fighter into Spyplane', describes the modifications to convert the Mark I fighter into a first-rate photographic reconnaissance machine. Chapter 7, 'The Quest for Range', describes the moves to increase the pitifully short range of the early Spitfire fighter variants. Chapter 8, 'Tailored for the Task – the Spitfire LF IX', shows how a relatively small change to the Spitfire Mark IX supercharger gave this variant a performance advantage over the German Focke Wulf Fw 190 fighter throughout the whole range of fighting altitudes. In Chapter 9, 'Production Flight Testing', Jim Rosser describes the procedure for flight testing Spitfires straight off the production line. Chapter 10, 'Spitfire Most Successful', recounts the service career of a Spitfire IX, EN398, flown in action by the fighter ace Wing Commander 'Johnnie' Johnson. Chapter 11, 'Spitfires with Sea Boots', describes the Spitfire floatplane variants, with comments by Willie Lindsay who was earmarked to lead a planned operation by these unusual aircraft. Chapter 12 lists the RAF and USAAF squadrons equipped with Spitfires early in June 1944, when the number of front line units operating the type was about at its greatest. Chapter 13, 'The Next Generation: Vampire versus Spitfire XIV', shows that although the Spitfire XIV was one of the fastest piston-engined fighters in the world, in terms of combat performance it was far outclassed by some of the first-generation jet fighters. Chapter 14, 'The Longest Spitfire Flight', describes the little-known but epic postwar delivery flight of a Spitfire XI to Argentina; the longest leg of that flight was 1,850 miles, the greatest distance ever flown by a Spitfire. Chapter 15, 'Deployment of RAF Spitfire Units: January 1950', reveals that even at this late stage the Spitfire still constituted a major part of the RAF order of battle. In Chapter 16, 'Cold War Warrior', Ted Powles describes the clandestine photographic reconnaissance missions he flew over the People's Republic of China in 1951 and 1952. Finally, Chapter 17, 'The Spitfire: Significant Dates and Superlatives', lists significant dates and events in the plane's long history.

Until the middle of the Second World War, Spitfire mark numbers used roman numerals. From 1943 to 1948, all new aircraft and new variants of aircraft carried arabic mark numbers, although the previous mark designations in roman numerals remained in use. As a convention in this book, Spitfire mark numbers up to XVI are given in roman numerals, and later versions use arabic. The RAF shifted postwar from using statute miles and miles per hour to nautical miles and knots. That convention is followed in the relevant parts of this book. One nautical mile equals 1.15 statute miles, and 1 knot equals one nautical mile per hour.

The story of the development of the Spitfire is far too long to be covered in a work of this size. Readers seeking a comprehensive account of the development of the Spitfire are recommended to refer to my book *The Spitfire Story* (Arms and Armour Press).

Permission has been granted to use the photographs and illustrations used in this book. Should any photographs have been unwittingly reproduced without permission, I offer my apologies and will make due acknowledgement in future editions.

Alfred Price
Uppingham
Rutland

FIRST OF THE FEW

Early in March 1936 the prototype F.37/34 (she had yet to be christened the 'Spitfire') sat in the Supermarine hangar at Eastleigh airfield undergoing final preparations for her maiden flight. The fighter's metal exterior was left unpainted, except for the RAF roundels on the wings and fuselage and the serial number, K5054, in black just in front of the tail unit. The fabric-covered control surfaces, the ailerons, elevators and rudder, were doped in silver. She was fitted with a fine-pitch wooden two-bladed propeller, to give optimum performance for take-off and at the low speed. The undercarriage was locked down and its fairings were not fitted. The aircraft carried no armament or radio.

From a collection of documents recently obtained by the R.J. Mitchell Museum at Southampton, which the curator kindly made available to this author, we can add several points of detail to the fighter's initial test programme.

On 5 March 1936, K5054 was wheeled on to the airfield at Eastleigh and comprehensively photographed. The maiden flight was to be undertaken by the Vickers parent company's Chief Test Pilot, Captain J. 'Mutt' Summers, but he had other important business that day. That morning he delivered the prototype Vickers light bomber, later named the Wellesley, to the RAF Test Establishment at Martlesham Heath. That task could not be rushed, for it involved showing RAF officers around the new bomber and generally 'selling' the machine to its intended customer. It was mid-afternoon before Summers arrived at Eastleigh in the firm's Miles Hawk runabout, piloted by Jeffrey Quill.

After brief preliminaries Summers climbed into the cockpit of K5054, strapped in and started the engine. When he was satisfied that all was as it should be, he waved away the chocks. He gave a burst of power to get the little fighter moving across the grass, as he sought to get the feel of the controls before taking off. The time was about 4.30 p.m.

From Meteorological Office records we know in detail the weather in the Southampton area that day: clear skies, visibility moderate to good and a light wind from the south-west.

Jeffrey Quill was one of those present, with Reginald Mitchell and most of his design team. He told the writer:

Mutt taxied around for a bit then, without too much in the way of preliminaries, went over to the far side of the airfield, turned into wind and took off. With the fine pitch prop the new fighter fairly leapt off the ground and climbed away. It then passed out of our sight but I know what Mutt would have been doing. First, he would have needed to confirm that the technical people had worked out the stalling speed correctly, so that he could get back on the ground safely. To that end he would have taken it to a safe altitude, about 5,000 feet, and tried a dummy landing to find the best approach speed and make sure that when it stalled the aircraft did not flick on to its back or do anything unpleasant like that. Probably Mutt did a few steep turns to try out the controls. Then, having checked that everything really important was all right, he landed and taxied in.

Before she took off on her maiden flight on the afternoon of 5 March 1936, the prototype F.37/34 (later named 'Spitfire') was comprehensively photographed outside the assembly hangar at Eastleigh. At that stage, K5054's metal surfaces were not painted. Her undercarriage was locked down and the undercarriage fairings were not fitted. Also, the aircraft had a fine-pitch propeller to give optimum performance during the take-off and at the lower end of the speed scale.

That first flight of K5054 lasted only 8 minutes, then Summers landed and taxied towards the knot of people waiting to receive him. Jeffrey Quill continued:

When the aircraft came to a stop everyone gathered round and he shut down the engine. Then, still in the cockpit, he said, 'I don't want anything touched.' Some of those present misunderstood his meaning and thought he had said that the aircraft was absolutely right as it then stood. As I know well, that was not the case. Mutt simply meant that he had found no major snag, the thing was functioning all right as a piece of machinery and he didn't want the controls or anything else altered before the next flight. Mutt was far too experienced and wily a pilot to say that

nothing would be needed to be done, on the basis of a single flight; he knew that the real testing had not even begun . . . But Mutt's comment became widely reported and equally widely misinterpreted.

From the recently discovered records we know that the fighter was altered in one important respect between her first and second flights: the fine-pitch propeller was replaced by one with a greater pitch angle, to take the fighter to a higher speed. Summers next flew the aircraft on the afternoon of 6 March, for 23 minutes. That confirmed his earlier impressions regarding its good handling, and took him to greater speeds and altitudes than before.

After the second flight, the fighter was returned to the hangar to have the undercarriage retraction system brought to operation and have the fairings fitted. Summers took the fighter on her next flight on 10 March, spending 31 minutes airborne on that occasion.

After the fourth flight, on 14 March, K5054 returned to the hangar for a series of modifications. Apart from the installation of a new engine, these were minor 'tweaks'.

The prototype was next ready to fly on the 24th, and Summers took her up for 43 minutes. On the following day Supermarine test pilot George Pickering took her up, and on the 26th and 27th Jeffrey Quill flew her three times.

During the final week in March, Jeffrey Quill and George Pickering flew K5054 in a series of runs to calibrate her airspeed indicator errors. Quill recalled:

These trials had to be flown early in the morning, because we had to have completely still air. We needed a straight measured course, so we used a section of the Portsmouth to Eastleigh railway line between two bridges. On each, we stationed a man with a stopwatch and they were connected by field telephone. Then I had to fly the aeroplane along the course very accurately, first at 100 mph indicated, then back at 120, and so on up to the maximum speed of the aircraft. From the readings taken by the men on the ground, we could work out the position errors and correct for them in our other test work.

During the initial flight testing the only serious fault with the Spitfire was that her maximum speed fell almost 20 mph short of the expected 350 mph. Almost as serious, but easier to put right, the rudder was overbalanced. That made the control too sensitive, and the aircraft was directionally unstable at high speed.

Early in April the initial test programme was complete and K5054 went to Farnborough for the mandatory ground resonance tests. These indicated that the new fighter was likely to suffer wing flutter at speeds somewhat lower than expected. As a result, for all future flights, K5054 had a never-to-be-exceeded maximum airspeed restriction of 380 mph (indicated). To overcome that limitation, the internal wing structure on production aircraft would be redesigned and strengthened but that of the prototype would remain as it was.

On 9 April K5054 returned to Eastleigh and went into the hangar for further modifications. Of these the most important was the reduction in the area of the rudder horn balance, by squaring off the top of the fin. The carburettor air intake was lowered slightly to increase the ram air pressure, and the engine cowling was strengthened to cure a rattle that had developed in flight. While in the hangar the prototype had the joints in the airframe filled and rubbed down, and she was painted in a smooth light blue-grey gloss finish.

At this time the Vickers parent company suggested, and the Air Ministry accepted, the name 'Spitfire' for the new fighter. Reginald Mitchell was less than enchanted by the choice, and Jeffrey Quill heard him comment, 'It's the sort of bloody silly name they would give it!'

Resplendent in her new finish, K5054 recommenced flying on 11 May. That morning Jeffrey Quill flew her for just over an hour for level speed and handling trials, and found that the re-balanced rudder made handling much more pleasant at high speed. That afternoon Mutt Summers flew the fighter for the benefit of John Yoxall, chief photographer of *Flight* magazine, for the first air-to-air photographs of the Spitfire. Jeffrey Quill flew the Falcon carrying Yoxall, and Reginald Mitchell went along for the ride.

Reginald Mitchell, the talented leader of the team that produced the F.37/34 design.

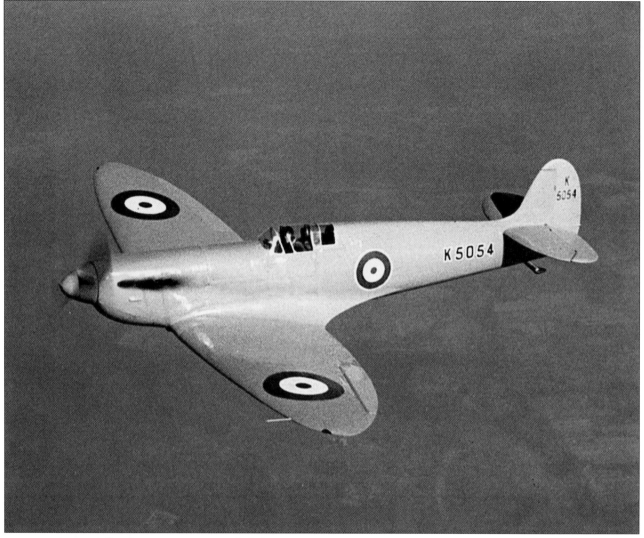

Mutt Summers flying the prototype on 11 May 1936, for the first air-to-air photo shoot of the new fighter. The aircraft had just emerged from the hangar, having been painted in light blue-grey overall and with the rudder balance reduced in area. (*Vickers*)

Quill flew K5054 again on the 13th, and then on the 14th he conducted a succession of high-speed dives to take her to her maximum permitted speed. On the first he reached 360 mph indicated, and found the aircraft handled perfectly. Quill pulled out, and climbed to 20,000 feet for the second dive. The speed built up rapidly until it reached 380 mph indicated, the maximum permissible, when suddenly there was a loud bang. Gently he throttled back, eased the aircraft out of the dive and returned to Eastleigh. After he landed it was found that the lower fairing on the port undercarriage leg had broken away. The loud bang had been caused by it striking the underside of the fuselage, as it fell clear. The damage was not serious, and after quick repairs the prototype resumed flying the next day.

Jeffrey Quill, right, took control of the Spitfire test programme a few weeks after the maiden flight. He remained in that capacity throughout the aircraft's long and eventful history. He is pictured with Ernie Mansbridge, who served as flight test engineer for the prototype and later variants of the Spitfire.

By the middle of May Supermarine was under pressure to deliver its new fighter to the Royal Air Force trials establishment at Martlesham Heath soon. The Spitfire's main competitor, the Hawker fighter later named the Hurricane, was already there. If the Spitfire did not begin her service trials soon she might fail to gain an order by default. But at that stage, the Spitfire remained stubbornly deficient in one vitally important aspect. Flight test engineer Ernie Mansbridge told this writer:

Even with the new finish and the lowered carburettor air intake, the best we could then get out of the Spitfire was 335 mph. From our 'spies' we heard that the new Hawker fighter was doing nearly 330, and

5 mph was not very much to justify production of the Spitfire which was obviously more complicated to build. Fortunately, our propeller people discovered that the tips of the propeller blades were running into Mach problems. So they designed and built a new one which paid special attention to that, with a thin section and a very fine incidence. The new propeller was fitted on 15 May and Jeffrey went off and did a set of level speeds with it. When he came down he handed me the test card with a big grin and said, 'I think we've got something there!' And we had, we'd got 13 mph. After correcting the figures we made the maximum speed 348 mph, which we were very pleased with.

On 26 May, Mutt Summers delivered K5054 to Martlesham Heath. Even at this early stage Supermarine's new fighter received special treatment. Flight Lieutenant (later Air Marshal Sir) Humphrey Edwardes-Jones commanded A Flight at Martlesham at that time. He recalled:

Normally a firm's test pilot would bring in a prototype aircraft for service testing, and it would be first handed over to the boffins who would weigh it very carefully and check that the structure was as it should be. It was usually about ten days before it came out for its first flight with us. With the Spitfire prototype, it was quite different. Mutt Summers brought her over, and orders came from the Air Ministry that I was to fly the aircraft that same day and report my impressions.

The new fighter was refuelled and Summers showed Edwardes-Jones around the cockpit, then the latter was ready for his first flight. As the RAF pilot later explained to this writer, it nearly ended in disaster:

Usually the first flight of a new aircraft did not mean a thing at Martlesham, they were happening all the time. But on this occasion the buzz got around that the Spitfire was something special and everybody turned out to watch – I remember seeing the cooks in their white hats lining the road. I took off, retracted the undercarriage and flew around for about 20 minutes. I found that she handled very well. Then I went back to the airfield.

There was no air traffic control in those days, and I had no radio. As I made my approach, I could make out a Super Fury some way in front of me doing S-turns to lose height before it landed. I thought it was going to get in my way but then I saw it swing out to one side and land, so I

knew I was all right. But it had distracted my attention at a very important time. As I was coming in to land, I had a funny feeling that something was wrong. Then it suddenly occurred to me: I had forgotten to lower the undercarriage! The klaxon horn, which had come on when I throttled back with the wheels still up, was barely audible with the hood open and the engine running. I lowered the undercarriage and it came down and locked with a reassuring 'clunk'. Then I continued down and landed. Afterwards people said to me, 'You've got a nerve, leaving it so late before you put the wheels down.' But I just grinned and shrugged my shoulders. In the months that followed I would go quite cold just thinking about it: supposing I had landed the first Spitfire wheels-up! I kept the story to myself for many years afterwards.

After landing, Edwardes-Jones telephoned the Air Ministry to give his report on the flight in person to the Air Member for Research and Development, Air Vice Marshal Wilfred Freeman. So far as Freeman was concerned, the crucial question was, 'Could newly trained RAF pilots cope with so advanced an aircraft?' Edwardes-Jones continued:

I took a deep breath – I was supposed to be the expert, having jolly nearly landed with the undercarriage up! Then I realised that it was just a silly mistake on my part. I told him that if there were proper indications of the undercarriage position in the cockpit, there should be no difficulty. On the strength of that brief conversation the Air Ministry signed a contract for the first 310 Spitfires on 3 June, eight days later.

K5054 now had her fuel and oil tanks drained, before being wheeled on to

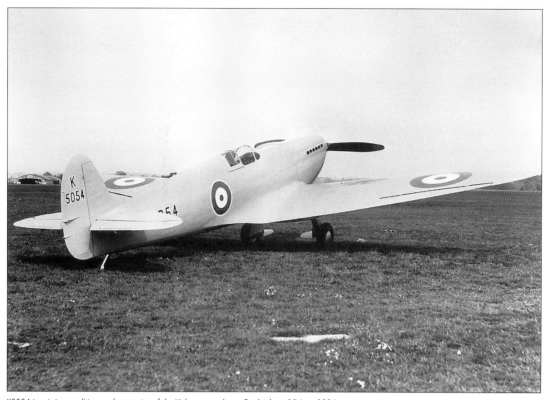

K5054 in pristine condition on the morning of the Vickers press day at Eastleigh on 18 June 1936.

Martlesham Heath's weighbridge. Her tare weight was measured at 4,082 lb. Then, with a full fuel load of 75 gallons, 7 gallons of oil, and ballast instead of guns, ammunition and radio set, plus an allowance of 200 lb for the pilot and parachute, her all-up weight was 5,359 lb.

On 6 and 8 June the prototype underwent further speed trials, flown by RAF pilots. They measured her maximum speed as 349 mph at 16,800 feet, or 1 mph greater than Jeffrey Quill had recorded. Earlier, Bill Lappin at Rolls-Royce had bet Reginald Mitchell £5 that the Spitfire would not reach 350 mph on the 990 hp from the Merlin Type C engine. On hearing how very close the Spitfire had come to achieving that target figure, Bill Lappin sportingly paid up.

The trials at Martlesham Heath continued until 16 June, when Jeffrey Quill returned K5054 to Eastleigh for the Vickers press day scheduled for the 18th. For the company the press day was an important occasion, enabling it to demonstrate its range of new products. In addition to the Spitfire there would be the Walrus amphibian, and the prototypes of bombers later to be named the Wellesley and Wellington. The Stranraer and Scapa flying boats would be displayed in the air.

When the time came for him to display the Spitfire Jeffrey Quill started the engine and taxied out. He opened the throttle to begin the take-off run and the Spitfire built up speed rapidly. Then, as he was committed to taking off, he noticed the needle of the oil pressure gauge suddenly drop to zero. That

Jeffrey Quill taxiing out to display the prototype aircraft at the Vickers press day. As he was about to leave the ground the oil system failed, and he was lucky to get the aircraft back on the ground before the engine seized. Had K5054 crashed, it is possible that that would have been the end of the Spitfire story.

placed him in an unenviable position. There was no room to bring the fighter to a halt inside the airfield, and in front of him on the other side of the boundary lay the built-up sprawl of the Southern Railway Company's locomotive workshops. Quill had no choice but to continue with the take-off, even though the engine might seize up at any moment. Once airborne, the pilot gingerly took the Spitfire round in a wide circuit on minimum throttle and was able to make a normal landing. Afterwards it was found that an oil pipe had come adrift and drained the lubrication system. The Merlin engine had suffered surprisingly little damage, but it had to be changed. For a second time the valuable prototype had escaped serious damage, or worse, by a narrow margin.

Fitted with a replacement engine, the Spitfire resumed flying. On 27 June Hugh Edwardes-Jones picked her up from Eastleigh and flew her to the Royal Air Force Pageant at Hendon, though he was ordered not to perform any aerobatics. Two days later Mutt Summers gave a rather more spirited display in the prototype at the SBAC display at Hatfield.

Following these demonstrations K5054 returned to Martlesham Heath. She was there on 8 July, when King Edward VIII visited the establishment and was shown over the RAF's latest aircraft, including K5054.

On 11 July, Humphrey Edwardes-Jones took the Spitfire to her greatest altitude so far, to 34,700 feet after a climb lasting 37 minutes. And there was a shock in store for him, as he later told the author:

In those days that was very high. It was the first time I had ever left a condensation

Inside the cockpit of the prototype Spitfire, showing the irregular positioning of the instruments. Production aircraft would feature the standard RAF blind flying panel, which was introduced later. (*R.J. Mitchell Museum*)

trail. I was horrified, I did not know what was happening. All that smoke coming out of the engine exhausts! Later, of course, they became quite common.

The sudden jump in fighter performance that came with the Spitfire opened several other areas of research. Humphrey Edwardes-Jones continued:

At about that time we had a 'G' meter fitted in the Spitfire, which was quite interesting. We did not know much about high-speed stalls and that sort of thing. We learned how much 'G' a man could stand without blacking out. During a dogfight with a [Gloster] Gauntlet we learned something not generally known at the time, how the stalling speed of an aircraft was raised when one pulled 'G'. Before aircraft like the Spitfire came along, one did not have sufficient power to pull sustained 'G' turns. The Merlin engine was so much more powerful than anything we had flown with previously.

For the rest of July the test programme continued, with a continual expansion of the fighter's performance envelope.

On 1 August, K5054 returned to Eastleigh for installation of the armament of eight .303-in Browning guns, reflector sight and radio. This was also the occasion to incorporate several minor modifications, including a new oil cooler and the installation of a parachute so she could undergo the all-important programme of spin recovery tests. Initially it had been hoped she would be flying again before the end of September. But then Rolls-Royce offered the promise of a new and more powerful version of the Merlin engine, the Type F, which developed 60 hp more than the Merlin Type C. The installation work imposed a further delay.

In the event, K5054 did not resume flight testing until 3 December. In the days that followed Quill carried out the programme of spinning trials, to test the fighter's ability to recover from spins with the centre of gravity moved progressively rearwards. There was a risk that the aircraft might spin at too flat an angle, and so fail to recover using the usual stick-forwards-and-opposite rudder technique. To guard against that possibility K5054 had a makeshift spin recovery parachute system, as Jeffrey Quill explained:

The small parachute, about 3 ft in diameter, was folded and housed in a box about 9 in by 6 in by 2 in, fitted in the cockpit on the right side. From the parachute a steel cable ran out between the front of the canopy and the windscreen, then to the base of the fin where it was attached to a ring bolt. To stop it flapping about in the airflow, the cable was held down at regular intervals with sticky tape. If the aircraft got into a flat spin and would not come out using the normal recovery procedure, the idea was that I should slide back the canopy, grab the folded parachute and toss it out on the side opposite to the direction of the spin (taking care not to let the cable pass across my neck if the parachute had to be tossed to the left!). The parachute would then stream out behind the tail and as it opened yank the aircraft straight, thereby providing what was in effect a much more powerful rudder. Once the parachute had pulled the aircraft straight, it could be jettisoned.

Quill tested the parachute and jettison system on the 11 December and found that it worked as intended. In the days to follow he flew K5054 seven times, with the centre of gravity moved progressively aft between each flight, and put her into spins in either direction. On each occasion the aircraft recovered normally, without having to use the parachute.

K5054 taxiing in at Eastleigh after a test flight.

After the Christmas break, K5054 underwent a series of trials worthy of Heath Robinson himself. On the prototype the whole of the external skinning was flush riveted, but that process was time-consuming and expensive. The company needed to know whether, on production aircraft, the simpler and cheaper dome-headed rivets could be substituted in some areas without a serious loss in performance. To find the answer, Supermarine engineers glued split peas on the wing and fuselage flush rivets where it was proposed to use the dome-headed rivets. The aircraft was then flown, and its maximum speed measured carefully. The split peas were then removed in stages, with a further speed run between each, to ascertain the effect. The results were startling. With split peas glued in position all over the

wings and fuselage, the drop in maximum speed was 22 mph, which was obviously unacceptable. However, with the split peas in fore and aft rows only on the fuselage, the speed loss was only 1 mph. The outcome of this trial was that production Spitfires would have dome-headed rivets in fore and aft rows attaching the fuselage plates, but flush riveting everywhere else.

Another change made at this time was the fitting of a tail wheel, in place of the streamlined tailskid. Humphrey Edwardes-Jones told the author:

The prototype had a most beautiful aerodynamically clean tailskid, which the firm was very proud of. The Air Ministry told them they had to replace it with a tail wheel, and the firm did not like that at all.

The tail wheel had been wanted from the start, but Mitchell thought it would spoil his design. What the Air Ministry had not told him was that the aircraft *had* to have a tail wheel, because they were planning to install concrete runways at service airfields. Using a tailskid on a concrete runway was hopeless.

After further testing, towards the end of February K5054 returned to Martlesham Heath for firing trials with her eight .303-in Browning guns. During ground firing on the butts, firing the full magazines, the weapons all fired perfectly. On 6 March the fighter climbed to 4,000 feet and, again with full magazines, the guns all functioned perfectly. On 10 March, Flight Lieutenant Dewar took off for what was intended to be the final armament test: firing full magazines of ammunition at 32,000 feet. That trial did not go as planned, however, and afterwards Dewar reported that only three of the eight guns had fired at all, as follows:

No. 4 port	171 rounds
No. 2 starboard	4 rounds
No. 3 starboard	8 rounds

The failure of five guns to fire, and the stoppages to the other three, were put down to the very low air temperature at that altitude (−53 °C) which froze the guns and the ammunition feed systems.

That was serious enough, but when Dewar touched down at Martlesham Heath after the test, the shock of landing released the breechblocks of three of the guns that had not fired earlier. Each weapon then loosed off a single round in the general direction of Felixstowe. That was obviously a dangerous state of affairs, and pending an in-depth investigation to isolate the fault and find a cure, the firing trials were halted.

Testing of other aspects of the Spitfire continued, however. Then, on 22 March,

K5054 suffered her first major accident. Flying Officer Sam McKenna was on his way back to Martlesham after a text flight when the oil system failed. Suddenly the oil pressure fell to zero and the engine ran progressively more roughly. McKenna switched it off and made a skilful wheel-up landing, causing only minor damage to the underside of the fighter. The damaged Spitfire was transported to Supermarine for repair.

During 1937 Reginald Mitchell's health deteriorated steadily, and from the beginning of that year he was able to spend progressively less time at his office. In March, an operation to arrest his cancer proved unsuccessful and the condition was pronounced incurable. On 11 June Reginald Mitchell died at the age of 42, a great loss to all who knew him. But by then his legacy to the nation, the fastest and potentially the most effective fighter aircraft in the world, had established its capabilities beyond reasonable doubt. Shortly after Mitchell's death, Joe Smith was promoted from Chief Draughtsman to Chief Designer at Supermarine and he took charge of the development of the Spitfire.

By September 1937, the repairs to K5054 were completed. The fighter now had a system to duct hot air from the radiator, to heat the guns and ammunition feed systems in each wing. When K5054 emerged from the hangar, she also carried the standard RAF camouflage scheme for the period of drab brown and green camouflage on the top surfaces and silver undersides. Several published accounts have stated that by this time K5054 had been 'modified to full production standard'. That was certainly not true. The differences between the hand-built prototype and the jig-built production Spitfires went far beyond what could be changed in a short makeover and a new coat of paint. Most significantly, the prototype's wing had a maximum speed restriction of 380 mph indicated (on

K5054 photographed on 22 March 1937, after Flying Officer Sam McKenna suffered an engine failure during a test flight from Martlesham Heath and made a forced landing. Coupled with modification work, the repairs would keep the aircraft on the ground until the first week in September.

(Above and overleaf) K5054 pictured after painting in camouflage drab in September 1937. Contrary to what some published accounts have said, she had not been 'brought up to production standard' at that time nor would she ever be.

production Spitfires with the redesigned wing, the maximum speed would be 450 mph indicated). Also, the prototype carried only 75 gallons of fuel (compared with 85 gallons in production aircraft).

Jeffrey Quill flew the repaired prototype for the first time on 9 September, and during the six weeks that followed he and George Pickering tested the aircraft with no fewer than eight different types of airscrew. A week later the Spitfire flew for the first time with the new ejector-type exhausts developed by Rolls-Royce. By carefully canting the exhaust pipes rearwards, engineers found they could get 70 lb of thrust – the equivalent of about 70 hp at 300 mph – almost for nothing. That increased the prototype's maximum speed in level flight to about 360 mph.

At the end of October K5054 returned to Martlesham to test the new gun heating system. Remote reading thermometers recorded the temperature at each of the outboard guns at high altitude. Although that brought about an improvement, the test showed that the ducting system did not carry sufficient heat at the guns to prevent them from freezing.

Other testing continued, and in February 1938 the prototype returned to Eastleigh for the installation of a modified system of gun heating. This employed 3½-in ducts to convey hot air from the rear of the engine radiator in the starboard wing to the guns in each wing. That method gave the best results so far, with satisfactory heating for all of the guns except the two outer weapons on the port side – those furthest from the radiator. To solve that problem it was decided to insert a bulkhead in the port wing out-board of the wheel-bay, to increase the effectiveness of the heating at the guns.

While these changes were still being considered, on 15 March the prototype suffered minor damage during a landing accident at night. The fighter was quickly repaired and within three days she was back in the air. During the next four days she made several climbs to high altitude to measure the temperatures in the gun bays, though the all-important inner-wing bulkhead had yet to be fitted.

Then, during night flying trials on 23 March, the Spitfire suffered serious damage in yet another accident. On landing, the port undercarriage leg tore away from the main spar, the result of metal fatigue in the port undercarriage leg. She dropped on her port wing tip and used that as a pivot as she swung round, causing damage there too. Yet again, K5054 returned to Eastleigh by lorry.

The repair work, coupled with the modifications to the gun heating system, lasted until mid-July. On the 19th, Jeffrey Quill again took her up. In the meantime the first production Spitfire, K9787, had made her maiden flight on 5 May. In the months to follow, the prototype's main role would be to test modifications being considered for production aircraft. Of those, the most urgent were those relating to producing a heating system for the guns that would be effective at high altitude.

On 27 July, K5054 returned to Martlesham to test the effectiveness of the new heating system with the additional bulk-head. That gave a further improvement, but still the two port outer guns received insufficient heating to prevent their freezing.

In September, the prototype returned to Eastleigh for yet more modifications to the gun heating system. On 4 October she returned to Martlesham for a comprehensive series of firing trials at high altitude. And now, finally, all eight guns fired their full complements of ammunition at high altitude with no stoppages.

With the successful completion of the gun-heating tests, K5054's part in the Spitfire development story was nearly at an end. By then, she had flown about 160 hours over a

period of 31 months. By modern standards that number of flying hours would be considered low, but it was about normal for that period. By the end of October 1938 twenty production Spitfires had flown, and henceforth all new modifications would be tested on one of these.

At this time K5054 was still one of the fastest aircraft in the world, and she could serve usefully as a 'high speed hack'. Accordingly, in November 1938, the prototype flew to Farnborough where she would spend the rest of her days. During the next three months she was engaged mainly in work associated with the planned attempt on the World Air Speed Record by a specially modified Spitfire (see Chapter 3). In addition, K5054 took part in tests of various combinations of fuel octane values, spark plugs and carburettor settings, aimed at obtaining the best performance from the Merlin engine.

After several close shaves K5054's flying career came to an abrupt end on 4 September 1939, the day after Great Britain entered the war against Germany. Flight Lieutenant 'Spinner' White had been testing some new spark plugs, but on his return to Farnborough he misjudged his approach. He came in too high, the aircraft stalled and bounced heavily a couple of times, then tipped on to the nose and fell on her back. Spinner White suffered severe neck injuries and died in hospital four days later.

K5054 was not repaired after the accident. Parts of her wings and fuselage went to the Photographic Department at Farnborough, where they were used to build prototype camera installations for reconnaissance versions of the Spitfire (see Chapter 6). The rest of the airframe was scrapped.

The prototype Spitfire had cost the British taxpayer £15,776. Rarely has government money been better spent.

SPITFIRE INTO SERVICE

On 15 May 1938 Jeffrey Quill took the first production Spitfire, K9787, on her maiden flight. Although *externally* she appeared to be almost identical to the prototype, *internally* she was a quite different aircraft.

Of the changes the Air Ministry required, the most significant was the strengthening of the wing's internal structure. It will be remembered that flutter considerations restricted the prototype to a never-to-be-exceeded maximum airspeed of 380 mph (indicated). After the internal structure had been redesigned, flutter tests at Farnborough established the never-to-be-exceeded maximum speed for the production Spitfire I at 470 mph (indicated).

Other major changes were incorporated in the first production aircraft: fuel tankage was increased from 75 to 84 imp. gallons; the travel of the wing flaps was increased from 58° to 90°; the cockpit instrumentation was revised to conform to the standard RAF blind flying panel; and two flare chutes were installed in the rear fuselage.

The first production Spitfire, K9787, with Jeffrey Quill at the controls, first flew in May 1938.

K9789, the third production Spitfire and the first one to arrive at No. 19 Squadron, pictured being examined by ground crewmen at Duxford.

Quite apart from the changes required by the Air Ministry, the company incorporated many others to ease the task of large-scale production. One such, mentioned in the previous chapter, was the use of dome-headed rivets to attach the fuselage plating. Moreover, several items that in the prototype had been hand-made from separate pieces were replaced by forged or cast items in production aircraft. Jack Davis worked in the Supermarine drawing office at that time, and he told the writer:

The task of redoing the drawings took about a year. One couldn't conveniently use prototype drawings for the production aircraft, there were so many changes. Though some of the production drawings might have looked the same as those for the prototype, it was much better to redraw and renumber the whole lot. I don't think a single one of the prototype drawings was used for the production aircraft.

As a result of the various changes, the first production aircraft weighed out at 5,819 lb fully loaded, 460 lb heavier than the prototype.

By the end of July 1938 there were two production Spitfires flying, both undergoing testing at Martlesham Heath. No. 19 Squadron at Duxford, operating Gloster Gauntlets, was chosen to introduce the new fighter into service. The first Spitfire arrived on 4 August, and others soon followed. Squadron Leader (later Air Commodore) Henry Cozens, commander of No. 19 Squadron at that time, described some of the difficulties encountered with the initial batch of Spitfires:

For one thing, the engines of these first Spitfires were difficult to start. The low-geared electric starter rotated the propeller blades so slowly that when the cylinder fired there was usually insufficient push to flick the engine round to fire the next; there would be a 'puff' noise, then the propeller would resume turning on the starter. Also, the early Merlin engines leaked oil terribly: it would run from the engine, down the fuselage and finally got blown away somewhere near the tail. Yet another problem was what we called 'Spitfire knuckle': when pumping up the undercarriage it was all too easy to rasp our knuckles on the side of the cockpit. There was a further problem for the taller pilots, who were always hitting their heads on the inside of the low cockpit canopy.

Modifications were in hand, or would soon be put in hand, to cure most of those problems. A more powerful starter motor cured the engine-starting problem. A new bulged canopy provided the some extra headroom to accommodate taller pilots. An engine-driven hydraulic system to raise and lower the undercarriage did away with the need for the hand pump and the resultant 'Spitfire knuckle'. These improvements were introduced on the production line early on. But the problem of leaking oil, though gradually reduced, would remain with the Merlin engine throughout its long career.

By October 1938, Spitfire production was running at about thirteen aircraft per month. Yet for its intended role the fighter remained deficient in one important respect: its guns could not be relied upon to fire at high altitude. At the time the Chief of the Air Staff, Marshal of the Royal Air Force Sir Cyril Newall, was stating no less than the truth

when he commented, 'If the guns will not fire at heights at which the Spitfires are likely to encounter enemy bombers, the Spitfires will be useless as fighting aircraft . . .'.

As recounted in the previous chapter, the revised gun heating system was successfully tested in October 1938. But not until the beginning of 1939, after about sixty of these fighters had been delivered, would this change be incorporated in production aircraft. There was then a programme to bring earlier aircraft up to this standard.

From then until the start of the Battle of Britain in July 1940, the Spitfire underwent numerous modifications to improve its fighting capability. The first seventy-seven production aircraft had been delivered with two-bladed fixed-pitch wooden airscrews. Subsequent aircraft were fitted with the de Havilland three-bladed two-pitch airscrew, with a fine pitch setting for use at low speeds and a coarse pitch setting for use at high speeds. With the new propeller the fighter's still-air take-off run was reduced from 420 to 320 yds, its maximum speed was increased by 4 mph, and its service ceiling raised to 3,000 ft.

In the spring of 1940 the two-pitch propeller was itself replaced with a constant speed three-bladed metal airscrew, either the de Havilland or the Rotol design. In flight the constant speed drive unit attached to the engine adjusted the blade pitch automatically, allowing the propeller to operate at its most efficient rpm setting for any given combination of boost and airspeed. The new type of propeller further reduced the still-air take-off run from 320 to 225 yds, and reduced the time to climb to 20,000 feet from 11 min 18 sec, to 7 min 42 sec.

In the spring of 1940, in a bid to further improve fighter performance, the RAF introduced 100-octane petrol in place of the 87-octane fuel previously used. In the case of the Merlin II and III engines fitted to Spitfires, this gave no improvement in

Squadron Leader Henry Cozens, commander of No. 19 Squadron at Duxford in the summer of 1938, pictured with a Gloster Gauntlet biplane. The unit operated this type until it had received its full complement of Spitfires. The Gauntlet entered service in 1935, had a maximum speed of 230 mph, and was armed with two machine-guns. The photograph illustrates the huge advances in aviation technology that were made during the 1930s.

Henry Cozens leading a formation of six of his unit's new Spitfires for the benefit of an official photographer in October 1938 (parts of the fifth aircraft are just visible behind the fourth in the line). The squadron number on the fighters' tails was not standard RAF practice and nor would it last; it was painted on the aircraft shortly before this flight and removed soon afterwards. (*IWM*)

performance at or above the engines' full-throttle altitude of 16,500 feet. Below that altitude, however, the new fuel gave a valuable increase in power. Supercharger boost could be increased from +6½ to +12 lb, without causing detonation in the cylinders. That increased the Spitfire's maximum speed by 25 mph at sea level and 34 mph at 10,000 feet. At altitudes up to full-throttle height, the fighter's climbing performance was also significantly improved.

Other modifications to the Spitfire at this time improved its fighting ability, though at some penalty to performance. To protect the pilot, steel plates weighing 73 lb were installed behind and beneath his seat. A thick slab of laminated glass on the front of the windscreen protected his head from rounds coming from ahead. Also, a 3 mm sheet of light alloy covering was fitted around the top of the upper fuel tank, sufficient to cause rounds striking at a shallow angle to ricochet off.

Another important addition was the installation of IFF (Identification Friend or Foe) transponder equipment. This enabled the aircraft to identify itself on the screens at radar stations along the coast of Great Britain, on which the Royal Air Force's fighter control system depended.

That series of modifications added about 335 lb to the Spitfire, and brought its all-up-weight in Battle of Britain trim to around 6,155 lb. Some of these changes also caused increased drag and had an impact on the plane's top speed. For example, the toughened glass slab in front of the windscreen cost about 6 mph, the IFF wire aerials from the fuselage to the tip of each tailplane shaved off another 2 mph. The maximum speed usually quoted for the Spitfire I is 362 mph at 18,500 feet. But that figure referred to K9787, the first production aircraft, during its initial performance tests in 1938 at an all-up weight of 5,819 lb. By the summer of 1940 the maximum speed of a

fully equipped Spitfire Mark I was somewhat lower, about 350 mph, at the same altitude.

While the .303-in Browning machine gun was reasonably effective against enemy aircraft lacking armour or self-sealing fuel tanks, the weapon was insufficiently powerful against bombers that had these features. The obvious answer was to change to a heavier-calibre gun, and the RAF selected the French 20 mm Hispano-Suiza Type 404 as the best available weapon of that calibre. The Hispano had a very high muzzle velocity, giving it an armour-piercing capability superior to any competing weapon. Plans were laid to produce the weapon in large numbers under licence in the United Kingdom.

In July 1939 the prototype cannon Spitfire (L1007), fitted with two French-made Hispano guns in place of all eight machine guns, underwent tests at Martlesham Heath. The extra drag from the cannon barrels and the bulges over the drum magazines reduced the fighter's maximum speed by about 3 mph. In other respects, the handling of the cannon-armed Spitfire was little different from the standard aircraft.

During firing trials, however, the cannon installation in the Spitfire suffered frequent stoppages. In the French Morane 406 fighter the Hispano cannon had performed well, mounted on top of the engine block and firing through the propeller hub. In that installation, the mass of the engine absorbed most of the hefty recoil forces. In the Spitfire the cannons were placed on their sides in less-rigid mountings in the wings, the only place where there was room for them. If the British fighter pulled 'G' while firing, the wing flexed and rounds would misfeed and jam. If the weapon on one side jammed, when the other weapon fired the unbalanced recoil forces made accurate sighting almost impossible. During the spring and early summer of 1940, RAF armament engineers devised a series of

small changes aimed at improving the reliability of the Hispano cannon.

By the spring of 1940 the prototype cannon Spitfire was judged to work well enough for this variant to enter small-scale production. Designated the Mark IB, the new variant entered service with No. 19 Squadron in June. In action during August 1940, the weapon functioned poorly and there were numerous gun stoppages. Clearly it had been introduced into front-line service prematurely. Following vociferous complaints from pilots, the cannon Spitfires were withdrawn from service for further modifications and they played no further part in the Battle of Britain.

One further simple modification introduced before the Battle of Britain needs to be mentioned here, the two-step rudder pedals. In normal flight the pilot placed his feet on the lower step. If he was about to pull high 'G', for example during a combat manoeuvre, he first placed his feet on the upper steps. That raised his legs by about 6 in and increased his 'G' tolerance by a useful amount.

By July 1940, when the Battle of Britain opened, the Spitfire I was a fast, effective and reasonably mature fighter that had proven its capabilities during the intensive if scrappy fighting to cover the evacuation of Allied forces from Dunkirk. It remained to be seen how well it would cope with the large-scale set-piece actions that would soon become the norm over southern England.

Spitfire Is of No. 19 Squadron pictured during the official press day at Duxford on 4 May 1939. The eleven Spitfires in the line all have the original two-bladed wooden airscrew, narrow aerial masts, ring-and-bead gunsights and unprotected windscreens. The second aircraft in the line has the original flat-topped canopy, though most of the others have the newer bulged canopy, which gave the pilots more headroom.

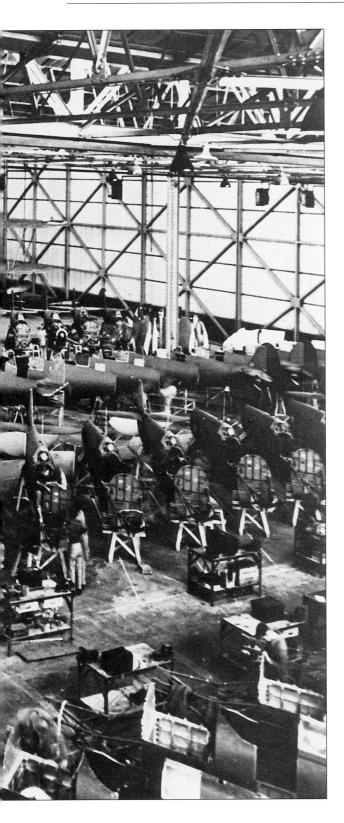

Production of Spitfire fuselages in full swing at Supermarine's Itchen works, early in 1939. In the background are Stranraer biplane flying boats, another of the company's products at that time.

Pleasing shot of K9795, the ninth production Spitfire, which was delivered to No. 19 Squadron on 27 September 1938.

K9791, the fifth production Spitfire, was retained by Supermarine and used to test various new features. She is pictured here fitted with a three-bladed Rotol constant-speed airscrew.

On 25 September 1939, Jeffrey Quill was airborne in test aircraft K9791 when she suffered an engine failure over Somerset. He selected a relatively treeless area near Weston Zoyland and decided to land there, if possible with the wheels down. As he neared the ground, however, he saw that the field he had chosen had dykes running across it. It was too late to select another field, so he left the wheels up and put the fighter down on the undulating surface where she suffered some damage. She is pictured during the recovery operation by Supermarine personnel. The aircraft was repaired and returned to the test programme a few months later. Note that the propeller fitted to this aircraft had wooden blades and it had been feathered before landing, a non-standard feature. (*via The Spitfire Society*)

Spitfire L1090 was shipped to Canada in the spring of 1940 and flown at Uplands Air Station, during comparative fighting trial against a US Army Air Corps Curtiss P-40 fighter.

CHAPTER 3

THE SPEED SPITFIRE

After the prototype Spitfire first appeared in public, in May 1936, the press hailed it as 'the fastest fighter in the world'. That led to consideration, both at company and Air Ministry level, to the possibility of modifying one of these aircraft for an attempt on the world landplane speed record. The world absolute speed record of 440 mph, held by the Italian Macchi-Castoldi MC 72 floatplane, was clearly beyond the reach of the new British fighter. Yet the *landplane* speed record, 352 mph, was held by an American Hughes H-I racing plane and that looked tantalisingly close to the Spitfire's maximum speed.

There were some problems to be overcome, however. At that time *Fédération Aéronautique International* (FAI) rules demanded that the aircraft had to fly over the straight 3-kilometre (1.86 mile) course twice in each direction, at an altitude not exceeding 75 metres (245 feet). The speed recorded was the average achieved during the four runs, to negate any advantage due to the wind.

During tests the prototype Spitfire had reached a speed of 349 mph, but that was at its full-throttle altitude of 16,800 feet. Low down it was flat out at about 290 mph. Clearly, the Spitfire would need extensive alteration if it were to reach the 355.5 mph needed – that is to say, 352 mph plus the requisite 1 per cent speed margin over the previous record.

In the summer of 1937, engineers at Rolls-Royce began work on a special sprint version of the Merlin engine. That August, a modified Merlin II, running at +18 lb boost and using a special fuel consisting of a mixture of straight

run gasoline, benzol and methanol, plus a dash of tetraethyl lead, achieved 1,536 hp. That was more than one-third greater than the standard engine was developing, running on 87-octane petrol.

Encouraged by this development and the prospect of yet more power from a further improved sprint Merlin, the Air Ministry issued a contract to modify two Spitfires for the speed record attempt, although in the event work was never started on the second machine.

The forty-eighth production Spitfire I, No. K9834, then in an early stage of construction at Woolston, was selected for modification for the record attempt. The project received the Supermarine designation Type 323, but more usually the aircraft was known as the 'Speed Spitfire'. Military equipment – such as gun mountings, ammunition boxes, the radio and flare chutes – was omitted, and fixed panels replaced the associated doors. To reduce drag, the aircraft had a shortened wing spanning 33 ft 8 in and more rounded tips. To dissipate the extra heat generated by the more powerful engine, the aircraft had a larger radiator and oil cooler. The modified Spitfire had a coarse-pitch four-bladed wooden propeller with a diameter of 10 ft, 8 in less than that of the prototype Spitfire. Compared with the normal one, the reduced-diameter propeller gave lower tip speeds at maximum engine revolutions, thereby reducing possible Mach effects.

The modified aircraft had a more streamlined windscreen and canopy, was flush riveted throughout and had a streamlined skid in place of the tailwheel. The modified aircraft weighed 5,490 lb, just

The Speed Spitfire in her original form. Note the streamlined windscreen and the much larger engine coolant radiator fitted to this variant.

The Speed Spitfire pictured during engine runs at Eastleigh late in 1938 or early in 1939. To get full power from the sprint Merlin engine the latter had to be started and warmed up using normal spark plugs. Then the engine had to be shut down for the fitting of the special racing plugs (see overleaf), after which it re-started normally. (*Flight*)

over 300 lb more than the standard fighter version.

The Air Ministry contract called for Rolls-Royce to prepare four sprint engines for the record attempt, two for tests and two for the actual runs. By November 1937 the company was predicting that it could get its sprint version of the Merlin to develop 1,995 hp. It was thought that this would be sufficient to take the modified Spitfire to 375 mph at low altitude. In that same month, however, the British attempt to take the world landplane speed record received a severe jolt when a much-modified German Messerschmitt Bf 109 had raised that record to 379.38 mph. That was 4 mph faster than had been predicted for the modified Spitfire, and it pushed the

minimum target figure for a new record attempt to 383 mph.

Despite that setback, there was still optimism that, with further changes, the Spitfire might still attain the required speed. In May 1938, Rolls-Royce ran its sprint Merlin at 2,122 hp, with a supercharger pressure of +28 lb boost.

On 11 November 1938, Mutt Summers took the Speed Spitfire on her maiden flight. Afterwards the aircraft was returned to the hangar for painting. All joints in the airframe were carefully filled and the aircraft received a high gloss finish with royal blue top surfaces and silver undersides. She had a silver lightning-flash cheat line running down each side of the fuselage and carried the Class B marking 'N.17'.

One peculiarity of the sprint Merlin was that to develop maximum power it needed to have special racing spark plugs fitted, but it would not run on those plugs when it was cold. The ground crew had to start the engine and warm it up using normal spark plugs, then they had the difficult task of carrying out a full plug change on the hot engine. Once that was done the engine could be restarted on the racing plugs, and would run at full boost.

Jeffrey Quill told this writer of some of the other foibles he noted when flying the much-modified Spitfire:

The Speed Spitfire had a special streamlined Perspex windscreen which was extremely bad optically. But one had to put up with such things in the interests of speed – think what it was like for the pilots in the Schneider Trophy contest.

With the coarse-pitch four-bladed propeller there was tremendous torque and one could not use full power for takeoff, one just used as much as was necessary. In the air at full power, torque could still be a problem and the aeroplane would tend to track sideways unless one flew it carefully and trimmed it out on the rudder.

Quill went on to describe the profile the Spitfire would need to fly when making the record attempt:

For the world speed record attempt the aircraft had to have a barograph fitted in the rear fuselage, and if it showed that during the flight the aircraft had gone above 400 metres (1,300 feet) – for example during the turns between runs – one was disqualified. It took quite a bit of time to wind an aircraft like that up to its maximum speed, about a couple of minutes. The initial acceleration was good, but at the very top of the speed range the

speed crept up only very slowly. So the trick was to get the aircraft flying flat out just under 1,300 feet, then ease down the nose to get a little more speed and cross the starting line at just under 245 feet going as fast as one possibly could.

Flight Lieutenant Harry 'Bruin' Purvis, the RAF pilot selected to make the record attempt, joined the test programme in February 1939. The maximum speed he reached was 408 mph at 3,000 feet, equivalent to about 400 mph at 200 feet. There were indications that the Germans were about to make a further attempt to raise the record, so it was imperative to squeeze yet more speed from the Spitfire. It was decided to dispense with the big engine coolant radiator under the starboard wing. It was calculated that with that reduction in drag, the plane's maximum speed at 200 feet would increase to about 425 mph.

Of course, the engine had still to be cooled or it would overheat and seize up. For that purpose the aircraft was to be fitted with a so-called 'boiling tank'. In place of the upper fuel tank, it would have a combined condenser and tank containing 62 imp. gallons of water. While the engine was running the water would be pumped through the engine cooling jacket and back to the tank, where some of the fluid would condense. The remainder would be ejected as steam from the base of the engine. Modified in this way, the Spitfire would carry only 37 imp. gallons of the special racing fuel. It was calculated that she would have sufficient fuel and water to take off, fly a short distance to the course, make the four runs for the record attempt, then return on the airfield. She had to be back on the ground before one or both liquids ran out.

Work to modify the Spitfire with the revised cooling system had just started when the Germans delivered another body blow to the programme. In March 1939 a Heinkel He 100 flew four runs over the course at an average of 463 mph, thus capturing not only the landplane speed record but also the world absolute speed record. Less than a month later a Messerschmitt 209 flew over the course at a blistering average of 469 mph, to create a record for piston-engined aircraft that would stand for more than 30 years. Those German successes robbed the Speed Spitfire of any prospect of securing a major world record, and with that the urgency left the project.

As proof of that lack of urgency, in July 1939 the Speed Spitfire was crated and shipped to Brussels for exhibition at the International Aeronautical Salon. She was shown with underwing radiator removed and the wing underside faired over, though the boiling tank had yet to be fitted.

Following the exhibition, the Speed Spitfire returned to the works at Woolston where installation of the boiling tank went ahead at low priority. It was the end of April 1940 before the aircraft was ready to fly again. On the 30th, Jeffrey Quill taxied out at Eastleigh when suddenly the cockpit was enveloped in steam. He shut down the engine and climbed out, and the aircraft was towed back into the hangar. There it was found that the boiling tank had developed a split.

During May 1940 the so-called 'phoney war' came to an abrupt end, and in the weeks to follow the Allied war position deteriorated rapidly. Desperate to get every Spitfire possible for the front-line or operational training units, the RAF conducted a trawl of trials establishments and other second-line units. The latter had to give up any Spitfires that were not engaged in work of vital importance that was closely related to meeting the current war situation.

The Speed Spitfire was a clear example of this, and Supermarine received instructions to bring her to a usable service condition as quickly as possible. The engine cooling system was returned to normal, and the aircraft was fitted with a standard Merlin XII engine with a three-bladed propeller. Because of the alterations to the structure to accommodate the boiling tank, however, she had room for only 60 imp. gallons of fuel. With her reduced span wing and exceptionally clean airframe, the Speed Spitfire was still one of the fastest aircraft in the world at a low altitude. However, she had not been built as a fighter and it would have required a disproportionately large effort to fit her with guns.

At that time the only front-line non-fighter unit in the RAF operating Spitfires was the Photographic Reconnaissance Unit at Heston (see Chapter 6). It was decided to send the much-modified Spitfire aircraft there. In November 1940, still resplendent in her blue-and-silver high-speed finish, but wearing service markings and the serial number K9384, the Speed Spitfire arrived at that unit. There she was fitted with a port-facing oblique camera in the rear fuselage, with the intention of using her as a high-speed low altitude reconnaissance aircraft. Wing Commander (later Air Marshal Sir) Geoffrey Tuttle, commander of the PRU at that time, told the writer what happened on the one occasion when he tried to use the K9384 for that purpose:

The range was ridiculously low – if you tried to photograph Brest from St Eval you would have run out of fuel about 20 miles short of the English coast on the way back. I took the aircraft out once to photograph a simple target in the Calais area, to see how it worked. And I had an absolutely absurd thing happen. As I was running in on the target at low altitude over the Channel I popped out of cloud to find myself in formation with a Heinkel 111. He must have been frightened to death,

Exhibited at the International Aeronautical Salon at Brussels in July 1939, the Speed Spitfire had the engine coolant radiator removed and the starboard wing faired over.

K9834 taxiing out at Benson in March 1942. At this time she had a normal PR Spitfire windscreen, in place of the more streamlined but optically poor racing version. (*Tuttle*)

but he needn't have worried, I didn't have any guns! I peeled away to get out of his fire in case he opened up, and had to re-align on the [reconnaissance] target. But even that small deviation depleted my fuel to such an extent that I was unable to photograph my target and had to abandon the mission. After that we used the Speed Spitfire solely as a runabout aircraft.

For the next couple of years, pilots of the PRU and at RAF Benson used the K9384 as a 'high speed hack'. From mid-1943 she became the personal runabout of the commander of No. 106 (Photographic Reconnaissance) Wing, Air Commodore John Boothman (who in 1931 had won the

Schneider Trophy outright for Britain). Some published accounts have stated that Boothman flew the Speed Spitfire over Normandy on D-Day, 6 June 1944, to photograph the initial landings. In view of the extremely limited radius of action of this aircraft, described above, those accounts should be treated with scepticism.

The Speed Spitfire survived the war, but not the peace that followed. With the disregard for important historical aircraft that was all too common at that time, she was sent to the scrapyard in June 1946.

Having followed the fate of one remarkable Spitfire, we now return to the Battle of Britain, which would be that fighter's finest hour.

Believed to be the only photograph to survive of the Speed Spitfire airborne, it shows well the reduced-span wing fitted to the aircraft. The picture was taken in mid-1943, when the aircraft was the personal runabout of Air Commodore John Boothman, who commanded the reconnaissance wing at Benson. (*Saffrey*)

Spitfire K9843 pictured at Benson in 1946, shortly before she was scrapped.

CHAPTER 4

FIGHTER COMMAND SPITFIRE UNITS

14 SEPTEMBER 1940

This chapter lists the strengths of Fighter Command's nineteen operational Spitfire squadrons on the evening of 14 September 1940, immediately before the action that was to decide the Battle of Britain. These units possessed 270 serviceable aircraft (figures in the main column), plus 70 more that were unserviceable (figures within brackets). On that date Spitfires made up just over 34 per cent of the Command's force of modern single-seat day fighters. Spitfire squadrons had an average serviceability of 79 per cent. That of the Hurricane units was 84 per cent.

To provide a complete picture of Spitfire strength at that time, this section includes those aircraft held ready for issue at maintenance units and also those serving with operational training units. It also gives the Spitfire production figures for the preceding week.

No. 10 Group, HQ Box, Wiltshire

Middle Wallop Sector

No. 609 Squadron	15	(3)	Middle Wallop
No. 152 Squadron	17	(2)	Warmwell

St Eval Sector

No. 234 Squadron	16	(1)	St Eval
Group Total	**48**	**(6)**	

No. 11 Group, HQ Uxbridge, Middlesex

Biggin Hill Sector

No. 72 Squadron	10	(7)	Biggin Hill
No. 92 Squadron	16	(1)	Biggin Hill
No. 66 Squadron	14	(2)	Gravesend

Hornchurch Sector

No. 603 Squadron	14	(5)	Hornchurch
No. 41 Squadron	12	(6)	Rochford
No. 222 Squadron	11	(3)	Rochford

Tangmere Sector

No. 602 Squadron	15	(4)	Westhampnett
Group Total	**92**	**(28)**	

No. 12 Group, HQ Watnall, Nottinghamshire

Duxford Sector

No. 19 Squadron 14 (0) Fowlmere

Coltishall Sector

No. 74 Squadron 14 (8) Coltishall

Wittering Sector

No. 266 Squadron 14 (5) Wittering

Digby Sector

No. 611 Squadron 17 (1) Digby

Kirton-in-Lindsey Sector

No. 616 Squadron 14 (4) Kirton-in-Lindsey

No. 64 Squadron 7 (3) Leconfield

6 (3) Ringway

Group Total 86 (24)

No. 13 Group, HQ Newcastle, Northumberland

Catterick Sector

No. 54 Squadron 15 (2) Catterick

Usworth Sector

No. 610 Squadron 14 (5) Acklington

Turnhouse Sector

No. 65 Squadron 15 (5) Turnhouse

Group Total 44 (12)

Spitfires serving at Operational Training Units, 14 September, 26 (24)

Spitfires held at Maintenance Units, 14 September

Ready for immediate issue 47

Ready for issue in four days 10

Spitfire production during the week prior to 14 September 38

(This page and overleaf) Jeffrey Quill conducting the production test flight of Spitfire P9450, in April 1940. At that time RAF home defence fighters had the underside of the port wing painted black and the underside of the starboard wing painted white, as an identification feature to prevent their being engaged by anti-aircraft guns. That scheme made the aircraft more conspicuous to enemy fighters, however, and it was abandoned in May 1940 when the undersides of fighters were to be painted duck egg blue. P9450 was issued to No. 64 Squadron, and remained on the strength of that unit throughout the Battle of Britain until she was lost in action in December 1940.

CHAPTER 5

SPITFIRE IN ACTION

15 SEPTEMBER 1940

On 7 September 1940, following a bombardment of RAF airfields in south-east England lasting nearly four weeks, the Battle of Britain entered a new phase. That afternoon several hundred Luftwaffe bombers attacked dock areas in the East End of London, causing severe damage and starting several large fires. In the week that followed the Luftwaffe mounted three further daylight attacks on dock areas near to the capital.

During each of those first four daylight attacks on London, the defending fighter force had failed to get to grips with the raiding formations. The initial attack had come as a surprise and the RAF fighters were positioned for yet another attack on their airfields. During the next three attacks, cloud cover had hindered raid tracking by ground observers and complicated the task of controlling RAF fighters. That produced a series of scrappy actions, with relatively light losses on both sides.

To Luftwaffe intelligence officers the sudden lack of an effective fighter reaction to compare with those during the August actions appeared to stem from a quite different reason: that the long-heralded collapse of RAF Fighter Command was imminent. If that analysis was true, the correct German strategy was to mount more large-scale attacks on London itself. These would force the surviving British fighters into battle, where they would suffer further losses from the escorting Messerschmitts.

In fact, despite heavy attrition during the Battle, by the second week of September Fighter Command's squadrons possessed almost as many Spitfires and Hurricanes as at the start of the Battle. The Command had lost several experienced pilots, but it had also received a steady infusion of new blood from other commands. New squadrons had formed using Polish, Czech and Canadian pilots. In addition, the force as a whole had gained considerable combat experience during the previous weeks' fighting.

For the fifth major daylight bombardment of London, scheduled for Sunday 15 September, the Luftwaffe planned two separate raids. The first, during the late morning, would employ 21 Messerschmitt Bf 109 fighter-bombers and 27 Dornier 17s with about 180 Bf 109s providing open and close escort cover. The fighter-bombers were to hit rail targets in the suburbs, and the Dorniers would attack the important conglomeration of rail lines and viaducts running through Battersea. In mid-afternoon a more powerful attack would be delivered by more than 100 Dornier 17s and Heinkel 111s, on warehouses and unloading facilities at the Royal Victoria, the West India and the Surrey Commercial docks. Every Messerschmitt Bf 109 unit in Luftflotte 2 was to support these attacks, with several units flying double sorties. Thus the stage was set for a day of fighting that would bring the Battle of Britain to a climax. This account will concentrate on the part played by the Spitfire squadrons.

Spitfire Is of No. 41 Squadron pictured during the Battle of Britain.

The first sign of an impending attack came at 11.04 a.m., when radar stations in Kent observed the raiding force forming up in the Calais–Boulogne area. From his underground operations room at Uxbridge, Air-Vice Marshal Keith Park commanding No. 11 Group ordered three squadrons of Spitfires and eight of Hurricanes to scramble and climb to 20,000 feet over their assigned patrol points above Kent. The three Spitfire squadrons (Nos 72, 92 and 603) headed for the patrol lines furthest forward, at Canterbury and Dover, where they would be ready to engage the raiders soon after they crossed the coast.

At the same time Park requested assistance from the adjacent fighter groups. No. 10 Group in the west sent one Spitfire squadron to patrol the Brooklands–Windsor area. No. 12 Group in the Midlands launched its 'Big Wing', with two squadrons of Spitfires and three of Hurricanes, to head for the capital.

At 11.31 a.m. the vanguard of the raiding force, a free-hunting sweep by about 60 Messerschmitt Bf 109s, headed across the Strait of Dover. The task of these fighters was to clear a path ahead of the bombers behind them. Park responded by scrambling six more squadrons, two of Spitfires and four of Hurricanes, to buttress his defence. With the exception of a fighting reserve comprising two squadrons of Spitfires and two of Hurricanes, held at readiness on the ground, his entire force was now committed.

The essence of good tactics is to exploit an enemy's weak points. To that end, Keith Park planned to fight the action in three phases. He knew that the attackers' Achilles heel was the limited radius of action of the Messerschmitt Bf 109 escorts. These carried sufficient fuel to allow only about ten minutes over London, at the most. The fighters assigned to close escort the twin-bombers had even less, for over enemy territory they had to zigzag to match their rate of advance with that of their slower charges.

The first phase of the action began shortly after the leading German formations crossed the coast. At 11.50 a.m. the forward deployed Spitfire squadrons sighted the incoming raiders. Their task was to try to engage the bombers, but if the escorts prevented them, it would still serve Park's purpose. It would force the German fighters to fly at full throttle, burning fuel faster than in the cruise and eating into their already slender reserves. It might also draw escorts away from the bombers, leaving the latter vulnerable to British squadrons attacking subsequently.

At 25,000 feet near Ashford, Flight Lieutenant 'Pancho' Villa leading the 20 Spitfires from Nos 72 and 92 Squadrons gave a brief radio call – 'Tennis Squadron, tally ho!' – to inform the Biggin Hill controller that he had the enemy in sight and required no further assistance. The Spitfires had a 9,000 feet altitude advantage over the Dorniers and 3,000 feet advantage over the escorting Messerschmitts. Villa dropped his right wing and arced into a dive. At measured intervals the other fighters followed. Accelerating rapidly, the Spitfires bore down on their unsuspecting foes.

From a Messerschmitt there came a sudden shouted warning call, the cue for the German fighter pilots to open their throttles wide and turn to meet their assailants head-on. Soon the sky around the bombers was a confused mêlée with fighters twisting and turning to deliver attacks, or avoid being attacked.

Sergeant William Rolls of No. 72 Squadron described how quickly fortunes could change during such a fast-moving action:

I saw an Me 109 coming down and it passed well over my head and appeared to be firing at the aircraft in front of me. As it climbed up again I climbed after it and at 200 yards, I gave a burst of about 2 or 3 seconds from underneath it. I saw a big black patch appear and several small ones on the fuselage. I saw some tracer coming from behind me as well and in my mirror saw another Me 109 coming down at me. I evaded it and could not get round to fire at it because it climbed away. As there were about twenty more above with it, I decided to leave it.

Shortly afterwards the twelve Spitfires of No. 603 Squadron waded into the fight. Pilot Officer MacPhail singled out a Messerschmitt for attack:

I turned and chased the enemy and got in a burst from astern. He turned to the left and I got another burst. The enemy rolled on his back with pieces flying off his machine and dived into the corner of a small wood a few miles south of Detling aerodrome and burst into flames.

The Messerschmitt crashed on Bearsted golf course. Those combats lasted only a few minutes, then one by one the RAF fighters had to break away as they had expended their ammunition.

Meanwhile the formation of twenty-one Messerschmitt 109 fighter-bombers and a similar number of escorts, flying at 20,000 feet, overtook the Dorniers. Those RAF pilots who saw the high-flying Messerschmitts took them to be a free-hunting fighter sweep, and left them well alone.

Keith Park's initial attacks had not succeeded in reaching the Dorniers, but the

Re-arming a Spitfire of No. 19 Squadron at Duxford during the Battle of Britain. The fabric covering over the wing gun ports has been blown away, indicating that the fighter had fired its guns. Under the starboard wing can be seen the empty or partially empty ammunition boxes which had just been removed. The rack in the foreground held two full ammunition boxes, ready to be clipped into place.

latter now faced an unexpected potential difficulty. On that day, in the band of altitudes between 16,000 and 20,000 feet over south-east England, there was a powerful 90-mph wind blowing from the north-west. The Dorniers advanced across Kent in the teeth of that headwind, and their crews discovered that instead of the expected ground speed of 180 mph they were making only about 90 mph. Thus, instead of the expected half-hour flight from Cap Gris Nez to the target, the bombers were going to take about twice that long. The Dorniers carried sufficient fuel to overcome the effects of the headwind but, as we shall observe shortly, the same could not be said for their escorting fighters.

As the Dorniers moved across Kent, Keith Park launched the second phase of the action. With an interval of about five minutes between each pair, eight Hurricane squadrons operating

in pairs were fed into the action. Again, the aim was to maintain pressure on the raiding force and cause the Messerschmitts to burn yet more of their precious fuel. For their part the escorts fought an effective blocking action, and although some bombers took hits none suffered serious damage.

The first raiders to reach the capital, at 12.05 p.m., were the high-flying Bf 109 fighter-bombers. Ignored by the defenders, they were allowed a clear run to their targets. After delivering inaccurate attacks on several rail installations, the Messerschmitts turned around and re-crossed Kent without interference.

For the Dornier crews, things did not go so well. Due to the powerful headwind, their escorting Messerschmitts had burned far more fuel than planned during their flight across Kent. The bomber crews watched in dismay as, just short of the capital, Staffel by

Pilot Officer Osgood 'Pedro' Hanbury of No. 602 Squadron pictured with his Spitfire at Westhampnett. Hanbury took part in the large-scale engagement near London on the afternoon of 15 September 1940, and was credited with the destruction of a Messerschmitt 110.

Pilot Officer Robert Doe flew Spitfires with No. 234 Squadron during the Battle of Britain, and was credited with 11 enemy aircraft destroyed, 2 shared destroyed and 1 damaged. (*Doe*)

Staffel their escorts turned for home. When the twin-engined bombers reached the eastern outskirts of London there was scarcely a Messerschmitt to be seen. The Dorniers were on their own.

AVM Park was probably unaware that the strong headwind had placed the Germans in this predicament, but had he known he would probably have acted no differently. He had concentrated twelve squadrons, with fifty-five Spitfires and seventy-six Hurricanes, over the eastern outskirts of the capital. As the raiders arrived there, the third and main phase of the engagement began.

As the Dorniers commenced their bombing run, they held tight formation as their gunners endeavoured to beat off their assailants. The bomber formation was only about 200 yards wide, which meant that the RAF fighter squadrons had to queue up behind to await their turn to attack. Early on, a Dornier suffered engine damage and began to trail behind the formation. Several RAF fighters attacked it, and it crashed beside Victoria railway station.

Meanwhile the rest of the Dorniers dropped their bombs on the rail junctions and viaducts in Battersea, before entering a sweeping turn to port to begin their withdrawal. That move converted the previous 90-mph headwind into a 90-mph tailwind, and the bombers re-crossed Kent with a ground speed three times greater than on their way in. But by now the RAF pilots were getting 'stuck in' to their opponents, as more Dorniers suffered damage and were forced to leave the formation.

In a typical action three Spitfire pilots, Flight Lieutenant Gillies and Pilot Officer Bodie of No. 66 Squadron and Pilot Officer Pollard of No. 611 Squadron, finished off one of the Dorniers. Their attacks had obviously left the bomber in a bad way, and 'Bogle' Bodie ran in for a closer look at the victim. Later he wrote:

He was pretty well riddled. Eight machine-guns certainly make a mess. I had a look at the pilot. He sat bolt upright in his seat and was either dead or wounded for he didn't turn his head to look at me or watch out for a place to land, but stared straight ahead . . .

The machine went on. The pilot was dead. He made no attempt to flatten out and land, but went smack into a field and the aeroplane exploded. I saw the pieces sail past me as I flew low overhead. I didn't feel particularly jubilant.

The Dornier crashed about four miles east of Canterbury.

Near Maidstone, the Messerschmitts sent to cover the withdrawal met the surviving Dorniers, leading to several venomous little confrontations between the opposing fighters. In one of these Sergeant David Cox of No. 19 Squadron became separated from his unit and decided to head south alone.

We were told that if we became separated from our squadron we should join up with any friendly aircraft in the area. After a few minutes, I saw six aircraft out to my right. They were flying north, in the opposite direction to me, not very far off. They looked like Hurricanes so I turned towards them, and they turned towards me. And then I realised they were Me 109s . . .

Two pairs of Messerschmitts passed underneath the Spitfire and that was the last Cox saw of them. The remaining two climbed, one went behind the Spitfire and the other went in front of it. Cox turned to meet the rear Messerschmitt, which bunted and dived away. Cox then made a quarter-turn and saw the other Messerschmitt about 600 yards away and a little above, about to fly across his nose. Aiming well in front of his enemy, the Spitfire pilot opened fire and saw

Close shave for Pilot Officer 'Bogle' Bodie of No. 66 Squadron, who had an enemy round stopped by his toughened glass windscreen. (*Oxspring*)

the Messerschmitt fly through his rounds. Then it turned slowly to port, the nose dropped and it descended into cloud. Possibly this was the Messerschmitt that made a forced landing near Uckfield after suffering damage to its engine cooling system. The pilot, unhurt, was taken prisoner.

As the surviving German bombers crossed the coast of Kent, the noon action ended. Six Dorniers had been shot down. Two more limped back to France and made belly landings, but were assessed as being damaged beyond repair. Nine Bf 109s had also been destroyed. For its part, Fighter Command lost two Spitfires and eleven Hurricanes. Now, at fighter airfields on both sides of the Channel, ground crews struggled to refuel and re-arm

their charges. The day's fighting was far from over.

There followed a lull of about an hour then, at 1.45 p.m., the leading aircraft in the second German attack wave came within the view of the British coastal radars. AVM Park reacted in much the same way as he had during the earlier action, though in rather greater strength. Six squadrons of Spitfires (Nos 41, 66, 72, 92, 222 and 603) were scrambled to patrol at various points, in pairs at 20,000 feet. Ten squadrons of Hurricanes, also operating in pairs, moved into position to intercept the enemy force as it moved inland. No. 10 Group dispatched one squadron of Spitfires and one of Hurricanes, and No. 12 Group scrambled its five-squadron 'Big Wing'.

Spitfires of Nos 222 (ZD) and 603 (XT)
Squadrons at Hornchurch during the Battle of
Britain. Note the steamroller in the background on
the left of the photo, to flatten bomb craters after
they had been filled with rubble and topped off
with earth.

At 2.10 p.m. the leading bomber formations crossed the coast at Dungeness, and wheeled on to a northwesterly heading that would take them to their targets. Shortly afterwards, the first of AVM Park's forward-deployed Spitfire squadrons went into action. The initial clash involved Nos 41, 92 and 222 Squadrons, with twenty-seven fighters. These immediately became entangled with the escorting Messerschmitts. Hauptmann Fritz Losigkeit of Fighter Geschwader 26, flying a Bf 109, recalled:

After we crossed the coast the British fighters came in from a great height, going very fast. They broke through to the He 111s ahead of us and below, to attack the rear of the formation. During the dive, some of the Spitfires became detached from the others. Using full throttle, my Staffel was able to catch up with them and I got into an attacking position. I fired a long burst and pieces broke away from the Spitfire's wing and fuselage. The pilot slid back the canopy and jumped from the cockpit. Overtaking rapidly, I pulled to the left of the Spitfire and saw his parachute open.

The Spitfire pilot was Pilot Officer Bob Holland of No. 92 Squadron, who was shot down at this time. He suffered minor injuries on landing.

By 2.30 p.m. all twenty-one of AVM Park's Spitfire and Hurricane squadrons, plus seven more from neighbouring fighter Groups, were airborne and had either engaged the raiders or were about to do so. On that day Winston Churchill was visiting Park's underground bunker at Uxbridge, and he watched the pattern of events as they unfolded in the operations room. Later the Prime Minister would write:

I became conscious of the anxiety of the Commander, who now stood still behind his subordinate's chair. Hitherto I had watched in silence. I now asked: 'What other reserves have we?' 'There are none,' said Air Vice-Marshal Park. In an account which he wrote about it afterwards he said that at this I 'looked grave'. Well I might. What losses should we not suffer if our refuelling planes were caught on the ground by further raids of '40 plus' or '50 plus'! The odds were great; our margins small; the stakes infinite.

Some postwar writers have suggested that Fighter Command as a whole was at full stretch at this time, but that was not so. When AVM Park told the Prime Minister he had no reserves, he referred only to No. 11 Group and the adjacent sectors. In fact, at that time, less than half of Fighter Command's serviceable Spitfires and Hurricanes were committed. The remainder, belonging to Nos 10, 12 and 13 Groups, would sit out the action at airfields in the west and the north of the country.

The German formation headed across Kent and, as during the morning action, it came under attack from successive pairs of Hurricane squadrons. Then, as the raiders reached the outskirts of London, the main body of Park's fighters went into action.

Flight Lieutenant Bob Oxspring, piloting one of the two Spitfire 'weavers' providing top cover for No. 66 Squadron, watched the unit's remaining nine fighters move into position for a head-on attack on a formation of Heinkels. Later he recalled:

While the others went in to attack, I was a bit concerned about some Me 109s above me and did a 360 degree turn to ward them off. I climbed to get more altitude in case there was a fight, being careful not to lose speed in the process . . . never get caught by the enemy at climbing speed, that is the worst thing that can happen.

The other Spitfires moved into line astern and attacked the Heinkels in succession from ahead and slightly below, where the bomber's defensive armament was at its weakest. Spitfire after Spitfire ran in to short range, fired a brief burst then broke away. From his vantage point Bob Oxspring watched the Messerschmitts above him continue on their way unconcernedly.

> They did not seem about to interfere so I went down after the rest of the squadron and attacked one of the bombers from out of the sun. With .303-in ammunition, you never knew if you had hit an enemy aircraft, unless you saw a flash or some obvious form of damage. The Heinkel broke away from the formation. I continued on, going down fast, and went through the formation.

Next, Spitfires of No. 72 Squadron attacked the same Heinkel formation, followed by two Hurricane squadrons. During one of these attacks a Heinkel suffered a lethal burst, it is not clear from whom, and fell like a comet trailing sparks. It crashed on open ground near Woolwich Arsenal. Two other Heinkels, less seriously damaged, fell away from the formation and turned for home.

Throughout the day cloud had been building up over London. By 2.50 p.m., when the main attack force arrived over the outskirts of the city, all the bombers' intended targets lay beneath a thick blanket of cloud: nine-tenths cumulus and stratocumulus, base 2,000 feet and tops extending to 12,000 feet. By chance there were clear skies over West Ham, however, and several Dorniers and Heinkels re-aligned their bombing runs on targets there. The Bromley-by-Bow gas works was deluged in a torrent of high explosive bombs and suffered severe damage. Elsewhere in the borough, an electricity sub-station was wrecked, cutting off supplies to many homes and businesses. There was widespread damage in residential areas.

The forty Dorniers sent to attack the Surrey Commercial docks found no target in that area, so they withdrew with their bombs still on the racks. On the way home they attacked targets of opportunity, hitting Penge, Bexley, Crayford, Dartford and Orpington, but there were few casualties.

During the bombers' homeward flights, the RAF fighter attacks continued. Leutnant Roderich Cescotti, piloting a Heinkel of Bomber Geschwader 26, recalled:

> Few Tommies succeeded in penetrating our fighter escort. I saw a Spitfire dive steeply through our escort, level out and close rapidly on our formation. It opened fire, from ahead and to the right, and its tracers streaked towards us. At that moment an Me 109 that we had not seen before appeared behind the Spitfire and we saw its rounds striking the Spitfire's tail. But the Tommy continued his attack, coming straight for us, and his rounds slashed into our aircraft. We could not return the fire for fear of hitting the Messerschmitt. I put my left arm across my face to protect it from the plexiglass splinters flying around the cockpit, holding the controls with my right hand. With only the thin plexiglass between us, we were eye-to-eye with the enemy's eight machine guns. At the last moment the Spitfire pulled up and passed very close over the top of us. Then it rolled on its back, as though out of control, and went down steeply trailing black smoke. Waggling its wings, the Messerschmitt swept past us and curved in for another attack. The action lasted only a few seconds, but it demonstrated the determination and bravery with which the Tommies were fighting over their own country.

The courageous Spitfire pilot was probably Flying Officer Arthur Pease of No. 603 Squadron who was shot down at a time and place, and in a manner, consistent with Cescotti's account. Pease was still in the cockpit of his blazing fighter when it dived into the ground near Maidstone.

The day saw numerous violent combats between the opposing fighters, though few of them lasted more than 20 seconds. Any pilot who concentrated too long on one enemy fighter ran the risk of being blasted out of the sky by another. This writer has found only one recorded instance of a protracted combat by single fighters on that day. Squadron Leader Brian Lane commanded No. 19 Squadron with Spitfires, part of the No. 12 Group 'Big Wing'. That afternoon he had to pull into a tight turn to avoid an attack by a Bf 109, then curved round to deliver his riposte:

He saw me as I turned after him and, putting on full inside rudder as he turned, skidded underneath me. Pulling round half stalled, I tore after him and got in a short burst as I closed on him before he was out of my sights again. That German pilot certainly knew how to handle a 109 – I have never seen one thrown about as that one was, and I felt certain that his wings

Squadron Leader Brian Lane, facing the camera, commanded No. 19 Squadron during the Battle of Britain. On the afternoon of 15 September, he took part in the only recorded lengthy one-on-one combat that day with an enemy fighter, a Messerschmitt Bf 109. (*IWM*)

Flying Officer Arthur Pease of No. 603 Squadron, whose lone attack on a formation of Heinkel bombers drew admiration from his foes. Immediately after the attack Pease was shot down and killed by escorting Messerschmitts. (*Sir Richard Pease*)

Spitfire P9386, Brian Lane's personal aircraft. Unusually, the aircraft had a yellow spinner.

would come off at any moment. However, they stayed on, and he continued to lead me a hell of a dance as I strove to get my sights on him again. Twice I managed to get in a short burst but I don't think I hit him, then he managed to get round towards my tail. Pulling hard round I started to gain on him and began to come round towards his tail. He was obviously turning as tightly as his kite could and I could see that his slots [on the leading edge of the wings] were open, showing he was nearly stalled. His ailerons were obviously snatching too, as first one wing and then the other would dip violently.

Giving the Spitfire best, he suddenly flung out of the turn and rolled right over on his back passing across in front of me inverted. I couldn't quite see the point of this manoeuvre unless he hoped I would roll after him, when, knowing no doubt that my engine would cut [due to the float-type carburettor fitted to the Merlin engine] whereas his was still going owing to his petrol injection system, he would draw away from me. Either that or he blacked out and didn't realise what was happening for a moment, for he flew on inverted for several seconds, giving me the chance to get in a good burst from the quarter. Half righting himself for a moment, he slowly dived down and disappeared into the clouds still upside down, looking very much out of control.

The sweat was pouring down my face and my oxygen mask was wet and sticky

Spitfire pilots of No. 19 Squadron who saw action on 15 September 1940. From left to right: Pilot Officer 'Jack' Cunningham; Sub-Lieutenant 'The Admiral' Blake, seconded from the Fleet Air Arm; Flight Lieutenant F. Dolezal from Czechoslovakia; and Flying Officer F. Brindsen from New Zealand. On that day Blake was credited with the destruction of a Bf 109 and a share in the destruction of an He 111. Cunningham was credited with the destruction of a Bf 109 and a share in the destruction of a Bf 110.

about my nose and mouth. I felt quite exhausted after the effort and my right arm ached from throwing the stick around the cockpit. At speed it needs quite a bit of exertion to move the stick quickly and coarsely in violent manoeuvres.

Afterwards Lane claimed the Messerschmitt 'probably destroyed'. His claim does not link with any known German loss, however, and no Bf 109 fell on land within 20 miles of Dartford where Lane reported that the combat had taken place. As has been said, long manoeuvring combats were rarities. More usually, fighter pilots engaging their

enemy counterparts followed the old adage of 'Get in fast, hit hard, get out'.

By 3.30 p.m. nearly all of the raiding formations had left the coast. The day's main actions were over.

During the two major attacks on London on 15 September, 192 Spitfire sorties and 327 Hurricane sorties made contact with the enemy. In those actions, eight Spitfires and twenty Hurricanes were destroyed. The eight Spitfires lost represented just over 4 per cent of the sorties they flew, the twenty Hurricanes lost represented just over 6 per cent of the sorties they flew. Thus a Spitfire making contact with the enemy had about a

During 1940, Spitfires carried out numerous night patrols. To assist with these the fighter had removable blinkers fitted on the engine cowling, to shield the pilot's eyes from the exhaust glare. This aircraft belonged to No. 65 Squadron and the pilot was Sergeant P. Mitchell. (*Glaser*)

50 per cent greater chance of surviving the encounter than a Hurricane, a pattern that was repeated in other major engagements during the Battle. The Spitfire's superior performance, particularly in the climb, meant it was less likely to be 'bounced' from above and made it a more difficult opponent for the German fighters. Also the Spitfire's fuel system was better protected than that of the Hurricane, making it less likely to catch fire.

During the two attacks on London, RAF fighters destroyed fifty-four German aircraft. Many of those fell to attacks from both Spitfires and Hurricanes. In other cases, the large scale overclaiming has made it impossible to determine exactly which RAF fighter type was responsible. Thus, it has not been possible to draw valid conclusions regarding the two fighter types' relative merits as destroyers of enemy aircraft. Probably they were about equal.

As has been said, a major contributory factor in Fighter Command's victory that day was the powerful wind from the northwest. Not only did this slow the raiding forces' advance on the capital and force many of the escorting fighters to turn back short of it, but it gave the defending fighter squadrons valuable extra time to climb into position to meet each raid. That greatly assisted the task of the fighter controllers. During the morning action Fighter Command scrambled twenty-three squadrons of Spitfires and Hurricanes, and all except one made contact with the enemy. During the afternoon action, Fighter Command scrambled twenty-eight squadrons of Spitfires and Hurricanes, and every one made contact with the enemy.

Towards the end of the Battle of Britain, the Spitfire II entered service. Manufactured at the Castle Bromwich plant, this variant was powered by the Merlin XII engine with cartridge starting but otherwise it was almost identical to the Mark I.

Although German losses on 15 September fell far short of the 185 planes the defenders claimed destroyed at the time, that day's actions effectively decided the outcome of the Battle of Britain. The German High Command was given the clearest possible proof that the reports of Fighter Command's impending demise had been greatly exaggerated. It was still a force to be reckoned with, and one that was unlikely to be defeated before the weather broke in the autumn.

With that in mind, on 17 September Adolf Hitler ordered that Operation Sealion, the planned invasion of England, be postponed until further notice. The ships and barges concentrated at ports along the Channel coast began to disperse, and from then on the threat of invasion diminished with each day that passed.

The Spitfire had demonstrated to the world its capabilities as a fighter plane. Meanwhile, with a lot less fanfare, one small unit equipped with modified versions of the type had shown that it could perform equally effectively in the reconnaissance role. This aspect of the story will be covered in the next chapter.

CHAPTER 6

FIGHTER INTO SPYPLANE

Before the outbreak of the Second World War, in most air forces long-range photographic reconnaissance was carried out by multi-engined bombers converted for the task. Compared with the opposing fighters these planes were relatively slow, and their need to carry guns and gunners for self-defence reduced their performance and increased the chances of fighter interception.

In 1939 a far-sighted but junior RAF officer, Flying Officer 'Shorty' Longbottom, penned a memorandum on the future of strategic aerial reconnaissance in which he proposed a radical and more effective way of obtaining photographs of targets in the enemy hinterland. His proposal centred on the idea of an unarmed, high-speed, high-flying reconnaissance aircraft that could dart into enemy territory, take its photographs and dart out. Rather than try to fight its way through the defences, it would avoid them by exploiting its speed and altitude. Today that concept is firmly accepted, but in 1939 it was a major departure from accepted thinking.

Longbottom went into some detail in his paper. He believed that the ideal aircraft for long-range reconnaissance was a high performance single-seat fighter, stripped of guns and radio and fitted with cameras and additional fuel tanks instead. Taking as an example the fastest aircraft then in service in the RAF, the Spitfire, Longbottom argued that by removing the guns, ammunition, radio and other unnecessary items of equipment, about 450 lb could be shaved off the fighter's weight. Like most fighter types, the Spitfire had a large reserve of engine power to give it a short take-off and a good

climbing performance. A long-range reconnaissance aircraft did not need a short take-off or a good climbing performance, so Longbottom thought it could safely be overloaded by up to 15 per cent without detriment to the performance parameters that really mattered. He calculated that a modified single seat fighter could carry cameras and extra fuel to a weight of 930 lb, and still perform effectively. Longbottom thought that such a reconnaissance aircraft might have a range of around 1,500 miles, and a cruising speed of 300 mph.

Longbottom's paper aroused interest, but at first there was no way of exploiting his ideas. In the autumn of 1939 the RAF was desperately short of high performance modern fighters, and each of these precious machines was destined for Fighter Command or the Air Component units based in France.

The pressure of war quickly changed official thinking, however. Within a few weeks of the outbreak of the Second World War, it became clear that the RAF possessed no effective strategic reconnaissance capability. Even during shallow penetration missions the low performance Bristol Blenheims, converted bombers, suffered severe losses from flak and fighters. And when these planes did return from a mission, in many cases they had suffered such harassment from the defences that they brought no usable photos of their targets. Unless something was done to repair this major deficiency, Britain's fighting services would have no reliable means of observing what was happening in enemy territory.

Following strong representations from the Air Ministry, Air Chief Marshal Dowding

Flying Officer Shorty Longbottom about to get airborne in a Spitfire PR 1A from Seclin, France, on 18 November 1939 for the first Spitfire photographic reconnaissance mission by a Spitfire. (*Green*)

reluctantly agreed to release a couple of his precious Spitfires for modification as reconnaissance aircraft. Two brand new Mark I fighters were sent for modification to Heston Aircraft Ltd, based at Heston airfield north of London. At the same airfield, Wing Commander Sidney Cotton was putting together a secret reconnaissance unit with the cover-name 'The Heston Flight', which was to receive the modified fighters. Appropriately, one of the first officers posted to the unit was Shorty Longbottom himself.

In the workshops at Heston the fighters had their armament and radios removed, and had a vertically mounted F24 camera with a 5-in lens fitted in the gun bay in each wing. The fighters' airframes were then 'cleaned up' to give the best possible performance. Metal plates sealed

the empty gun ports, all joints were filled with plaster of Paris and rubbed down to give a smooth exterior finish. It was necessary to explore the new operational concept as soon as possible, to see if it was workable. For that reason, the first reconnaissance Spitfires had a minimum of modification, and carried no additional fuel tanks.

In the autumn of 1939 Cotton's unit was renamed 'No. 2 Camouflage Unit', and in November it sent an aircraft to Seclin near Lille in France to carry out operational tests of the Spitfire in the reconnaissance role. On the 18th, Shorty Longbottom, recently promoted to Flight Lieutenant, took the Spitfire on its first reconnaissance mission. His brief was to photograph the fortifications outside the German city of Aachen, but as he ran through the area at 33,000 feet he found that navigation was much more difficult than expected. During photography, it was important that the Spitfire's wings were horizontal – a few degrees of bank would point the cameras away from the target. Yet, with the wings horizontal, there was no view of the ground below or for quite a long way on either side. When Longbottom's films were developed, they showed a strip of ground on the Belgian side of the frontier south of Aachen with no sign of the German fortifications.

Longbottom quickly worked out a way to circumvent the problem. During his next photographic mission, on 22 November, he navigated the Spitfire using ground features more than ten miles away on either side of his intended track. Using this technique he navigated accurately, and returned with high altitude photographs of the defences along the Belgian–German border to the east of Liege.

During the six weeks following those initial flights, long periods of cloud cover prevented high altitude photography of enemy territory. Only at the end of December did the skies clear sufficiently to allow the reconnaissance Spitfires to resume operations. In short order they photographed Aachen, Cologne, Kaiserslautern, Wiesbaden, Mainz and parts of the Ruhr.

By the end of 1939, the two Spitfires had flown fifteen sorties without loss. Two-thirds of the sorties had yielded photographs of enemy territory. Five sorties had had to be aborted, of which four were due to cloud cover and only one was due to enemy interference. Those initial operations demonstrated that the Spitfire could reach targets well inside enemy territory, photograph them and return with little risk of interception. It was unfortunate, therefore, that the photographs brought back so far had showed so little of military value.

The fundamental problem was that the Spitfire's high altitude performance greatly

exceeded the performance of the available aerial cameras. In 1939 the standard RAF reconnaissance camera, the F24 with a 5-in lens, had been designed to photograph targets from altitudes not much greater than 10,000 feet. From there the camera produced photographs with a scale of 1:24,000; that is to say, 1 inch on the print represented 666 yards on the ground. That scale was sufficiently small to allow interpreters to identify troop positions, and pick out individual vehicles and military installations on the prints.

When that same camera was used to take photographs from 30,000 feet, the latter had a scale of 1:72,000; that is to say, 1 inch on the print represented just over a mile on the ground. That was far too large a scale for the interpreters to extract much useful intelligence from the pictures. Enlarging the prints would not solve the problem because the sort of detail required – troop positions, individual vehicles, bomb damage, etc. – was about the same size as the grain of the film and could not be seen using magnification.

During January 1940 an improved photographic reconnaissance Spitfire emerged from the workshop at Heston, designated the PR IB (to differentiate them, the two earlier reconnaissance versions were now designated as PR IAs). Like its predecessor, the PR IB carried a pair of F24 cameras in the wings, but on the new variant they had 8-in lenses. The longer lens gave a small but useful improvement in the scale of photographs taken from 30,000 feet: 1:45,000, or 1 inch on the print, equalled three-quarters of a mile on the ground. To increase its range, the PR IB carried an extra 29-gallon fuel tank in the rear fuselage.

Shorty Longbottom demonstrated the value of the PR IB in February 1940 when, during a single sortie, he photographed the important German naval bases at Wilhelmshaven and Emden. In the following

Spitfire reconnaissance pilots in France, 1940. Second from the right is 'Shorty' Longbottom, one of the key players in establishing the Spitfire in the photographic reconnaissance role. (*Tuttle*)

month, one of these aircraft photographed almost the whole of the Ruhr industrial area in a single flight. A mosaic, assembled from prints taken during that sortie, would become a standard briefing aid for crews flying over that strategically important area for the rest of the war.

Early in 1940 Cotton's unit was renamed once more, and it became the Photographic Development Unit (PDU). For the first time, the unit's title indicated the nature of its activities. Soon afterwards the RAF formalised its reconnaissance operation in France with the creation of a new unit, No. 212 Squadron. The unit operated reconnaissance Spitfires and Blenheims, and was based at Seclin.

In the mean time, the workshop at Heston had produced a further upgrade of the reconnaissance Spitfire. The PR IC appeared in March 1940, fitted with a 30-gallon blister tank under the port wing. A pair of cameras counterbalanced that with 8-in lenses in a similar blister under the starboard wing. With 29 gallons of extra fuel in a tank in the rear fuselage, this version carried 59 gallons of fuel more than the fighter version.

The extra range was soon put to good use. On 7 April 1940, Shorty Longbottom flew the prototype PR IC to photograph the harbour at Kiel. His photographs revealed considerable military activity in the area, with numerous ships in the harbour and lines of Junkers 52 transport planes at the nearby Holtenau airfield. There had been no previous photography of either the port or the airfield for comparison, so it was impossible to know whether that degree of activity was normal or if a large-scale military operation was in the offing. Two days later the significance of concentrations became clear, when German troops invaded Denmark and Norway. The Kiel incident highlighted the importance of conducting a regular aerial reconnaissance of important targets, so that changes in the enemy's dispositions would be readily apparent.

On 10 May 1940, just over a month later, German forces launched their all-out offensive in the west. In the hectic days that followed, the Spitfires of No. 212 Squadron brought back scores of photographs showing advancing German troops and the roads behind them packed with follow-up units. The Panzers thrust forward in great strength, driving a wedge through the defending forces and destroying or bypassing Allied strongpoints in their path. Finally, they reached the English Channel near Abbeville to split the Allied armies into two.

The Spitfires' photographs could not avert the Allies' impending defeat. Nevertheless, they were to play a vital role in the unfolding pattern of events. They left Allied

commanders with no illusions regarding the desperate nature of their rapidly worsening predicament. That led to a timely start to preparations for what would become the successful evacuation of Allied troops from Dunkirk. It is no exaggeration to say that the intelligence collected on enemy dispositions by the reconnaissance Spitfires was instrumental in preventing the defeat in France from turning into an unmitigated disaster.

In the final stages of the battle of France No. 212 Squadron withdrew to England, where its surviving aircraft and personnel were incorporated into the PDU at Heston. In July 1940, Wing Commander Geoffrey Tuttle replaced Sidney Cotton as commander of the unit, and the PDU changed its name yet again to the Photographic Reconnaissance Unit (PRU). The changes of commander and its name made no difference to the way the unit operated, however.

In July 1940 a further Spitfire reconnaissance variant made its debut, the PR IF. This carried a 29-gallon tank behind the pilot and a 30-gallon blister tank under each wing, giving it 89 gallons of extra fuel or more than double that carried by the fighter version. Also, the new variant carried an enlarged oil tank beneath the engine. Mounted in the rear fuselage, the camera installation comprised two F24s, initially with 8-in lenses, later with 20-in lenses. The latter gave a further improvement in the scale of photographs (1:18,000 for shots taken from 30,000 feet). The additional fuel increased the radius of action of the PR IF by about 100 miles, compared with the PR IC.

Throughout the summer and autumn of 1940, reconnaissance Spitfires maintained a close watch on German preparations for the invasion of Britain. At this time the PRU, comparable in strength to a normal RAF fighter squadron, made a contribution to the national defence far greater than any other unit of similar size. On each day when the

This Spitfire PR 1B was left behind at Rheims/Champagne when No. 212 Squadron withdrew from France in June 1940, and fell intact into German hands.

weather allowed, its Spitfires photographed every German-held port along the Channel Coast. Interpreters were thus able to make regular and accurate counts of the numbers of ships and barges assembled at each port, providing vital intelligence on the state of the invasion preparations.

By now the British cipher breakers at Bletchley Park were decrypting a growing number of German high-grade signals, in an operation code-named 'Ultra'. That source produced a steady stream of useful information on German plans and deployments. Because it was vitally important to preserve the security of

that intelligence source, it was ruled that information secured through Ultra could not be used unless it might reasonably have been obtained from another quarter. Growing numbers of Spitfire reconnaissance sorties were flown as a back-up for Ultra decrypts, unknown to the pilots involved. Once a British reconnaissance aircraft had passed over a particular area, the Germans had to assume that the British had knowledge of any activity or concentration of forces there.

Following the great air action on 15 September 1940, described in the previous chapter, Adolf Hitler ordered that the

Spitfire PR 1C seen with the camera door open and an airman unloading the film magazines. (*Green*)

PR 1C taxiing in after a mission, showing the rounded fuel tank under the port wing and the flat camera window on the bulge under the starboard wing. (*Tuttle*)

Spitfire PR 1F being pushed into its dispersal point at St Eval, Cornwall, after a sortie.

invasion be postponed until the following year. On 20 September, in a follow-up to an Ultra intercept, a reconnaissance Spitfire returned from Cherbourg with photographic confirmation that five destroyers and a torpedo boat had left the port. Successive photographic sorties in the weeks to follow revealed steady reductions in the numbers of ships and barges assembled at the various ports. The threat of invasion had passed, never to be resumed.

The Type C and Type F Spitfires kept a useful area of enemy territory under surveillance, but in October 1940 the Supermarine Company showed that even more range could be obtained from its design. The wing leading edge was redesigned to house a huge integral fuel tank with a capacity of 114 gallons. The new Spitfire variant with this feature, designated the PR

ID, also carried a 29-gallon tank in the rear fuselage. These changes gave the aircraft a total internal fuel capacity of 228 gallons – two and a half times more than the standard Mark I fighter. The camera installation, housed in the rear fuselage, comprised two F24s with 8-in or 20-in focal length lenses. After a year of incremental improvements, here at last was a reconnaissance Spitfire that came close to 'Shorty' Longbottom's original concept for such an aircraft.

The PR ID soon demonstrated its prowess. On 29 October 1940, one of these aircraft photographed the port of Stettin on the Baltic (now Sczecin in Poland). Other remarkable missions soon followed: to Marseilles and Toulon in the south of France, and to Trondheim in Norway.

While the range performance of the PR ID was spectacular, it was not an easy aircraft to

Close-up of the fixed blister fuel tank under the port wing of a PR IF.

The Spitfire PR 1D had no underwing tanks or bulges; it carried its extra fuel in a large integral tank built into the leading edge of the wing and its cameras in the rear fuselage behind the cockpit.

fly when it carried its full load of fuel. Flight Lieutenant (later Air Chief Marshal Sir) Neil Wheeler, one of the early Spitfire reconnaissance pilots, told the writer:

> You could not fly it straight and level for the first half hour or hour after take-off. Until you had emptied the rear tank, the aircraft hunted the whole time. The centre of gravity was so far back that you couldn't control it. It was the sort of thing that would never have got in during peacetime, but war is another matter.

As the rear fuel tank drained, the Spitfire's normally pleasant handling characteristics gradually returned.

At altitudes around 30,000 feet the outside air temperature varied between -30 °C and -50 °C. On very long-range missions that often lasted more than five hours, the lack of an effective cockpit heating system in the early Spitfires caused considerable discomfort. Neil Wheeler continued:

> I found the extreme cold most uncomfortable. On my feet, I wore a pair of ladies' silk stockings, a pair of football stockings, a pair of oiled Scandinavian ski socks and RAF fur-lined boots. On my hands, I wore two pairs of RAF silk gloves and some special fur-backed-and-lined gauntlets which I had to buy for myself. It was essential to retain some fingertip control, particularly for the camera control box. Otherwise, I wore normal uniform [RAF battledress had not been invented in 1940] with a thick vest, roll-neck sweater and a thing called a Tropal lining which was stuffed with a form of kapok.

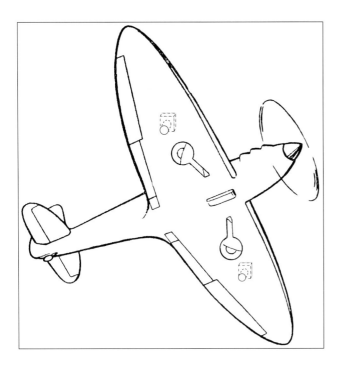

(Left) Spitfire PR 1A. Vertically mounted F24 camera with 5-in lens in each wing, no additional fuel tanks.

(Right) Spitfire PR 1B. Vertically mounted F24 lens with 8-in lens in each wing, 29-gallon fuel tank immediately behind the pilot.

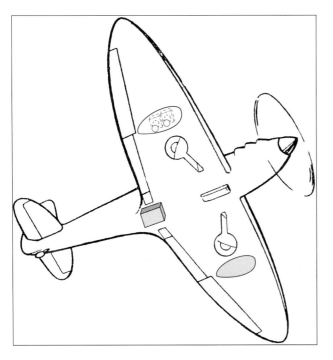

(Left) Spitfire PR 1C. Two vertically mounted F24 cameras with 8-in lenses in blister under starboard wing, 30-gallon fuel tank in blister under port wing, 29-gallon fuel tank immediately behind the pilot.

(Right) Spitfire PR 1D. Two vertically mounted F24 cameras with 8-in or 20-in lenses in rear fuselage. Integral tanks for 114 gallons of extra fuel in the leading edge of the wings, 29-gallon fuel tank immediately behind the pilot.

(Left) Spitfire PR 1E. One oblique F24 camera with 14-in lens in blister under either wing, facing 90 degrees to the line of flight and slightly down. Probably carried a 29-gallon fuel tank immediately behind the pilot.

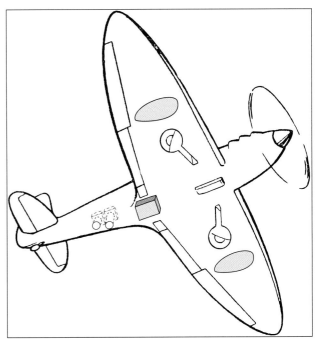

(Right) Spitfire PR 1F. Two vertically mounted F24 cameras with 8-in or 20-in lenses in rear fuselage, 30-gallon tank in blisters under each wing, 29-gallon fuel tank immediately behind the pilot.

Spitfire PR 1G. Cameras in rear fuselage: one obliquely mounted F24 camera with 14-in lens looking either to port or to starboard; two vertically mounted F24s, one with a 14-in lens and one with a 5-in lens. One 29-gallon fuel tank immediately behind the pilot. Aircraft retained fighter armament of eight .303-in machine-guns.

In all the early reconnaissance Spitfires the cameras were mounted vertically, and pilots photographed their targets from vertically above. In mid-1940 a new technique was developed, that of using a fixed oblique camera to take close-up photographs of a small target from low altitude. The first variant with an oblique camera installation was the PR IE. This had a streamlined fairing under each wing housing an F24 camera with a 5-in lens. The latter pointed outwards at right angles to the line of flight, and looked 13 degrees below the horizontal. That installation was not successful, however, and only one PR IE was so modified. To replace it came the PR IG, whose camera installation was carried in the rear fuselage and comprised a 5-in oblique camera looking to port or starboard, and 14-in and 5-in lens camera mounted vertically. To extend its range, this variant carried a 29-gallon fuel tank in the rear fuselage. Also, to provide a self-defence capability if it encountered enemy fighters, the PR IG retained the fighter's armament of eight .303-in machine guns.

The low altitude photography missions comprised only a small proportion of the reconnaissance effort, but they were the most dangerous for the pilots involved. Most PR IGs were painted a very pale shade of pink, barely off-white, which effectively concealed them if they flew immediately below a layer of cloud. If the aircraft came under fire from AA guns the pilot climbed into cloud, then changed heading and made good his escape. If there was no cloud cover above the aircraft, however, it would have been suicidal to fly such a conspicuous plane over enemy territory. Pilots flying pink Spitfires therefore had orders to abandon their mission if they did not have the requisite degree of cloud cover above them.

In November 1940 the Photographic Reconnaissance Unit was redesignated No. 1 Photographic Reconnaissance Unit, to distinguish it from No. 2 Photographic

The PR IG was optimised for low altitude photographic missions below cloud, with an oblique camera pointing to port and two vertical cameras all carried in the rear fuselage. This variant was usually painted pale pink overall, and it retained its armament of eight .303-in machine guns. (*Green*)

Reconnaissance Unit forming in the Mediterranean theatre. Soon afterwards, No. 1 PRU moved from Heston to Benson near Oxford, which then became the hub of RAF reconnaissance operations for the remainder of the war.

During 1941, the RAF rationalised its system of designating the reconnaissance Spitfires. The PR Type D became the PR Mark IV; the Type F became the PR Mark VI and the Type G became the PR Mark VII (by then the earlier reconnaissance Spitfire variants that survived had been modified into Type Fs or Gs, or had passed out of service). Also during that year all reconnaissance Spitfires in front line service were fitted or retrofitted with the more powerful Merlin 45 series engine. With the new engine came a modification that

would do much to improve the morale of reconnaissance pilots: the installation of an effective cabin heating system.

During their first couple of years of reconnaissance operations, the Spitfire pilots built up a wealth of experience in this type of work. Pilot Officer (later Air Vice Marshal Sir) Alfred Ball recalled:

First and foremost, we always flew alone and far from the madding crowd which encouraged a very independent and individualistic frame of mind – it was the ideal job for a 'loner'. The pilot was given his targets and any possible alternatives adjacent to his track in case he had film left over or cloud covered his main targets; he was then left to plan his routes and

Close-up of a PR IG with reconnaissance ace Flight Lieutenant Gordon Hughes by the cockpit. The window for the oblique camera can be see immediately to the left of the fuselage roundel. Note the bulge mounted on the side of the cockpit canopy, a feature of the early reconnaissance Spitfires to improve the view downwards and to the rear. (*Tuttle*)

methods as he wished. He was on his own for long periods, five or six hours on the longer sorties; the one thing he did not want was to meet other aircraft – enemy or friendly produced the same reaction when one met them in the middle of Germany. One of my worst frights occurred when a fighter came out of the sun and passed 50 feet away going in the opposite direction near Munich – it was another blue Spitfire!

Low level oblique photograph of a Wassermann long-range early warning radar on the coast near Bergen in Holland, taken from a Spitfire.

Spitfire PR IVs (alias PR IDs) being assembled in the small hangar at Henley airfield.

In 1942 the Luftwaffe deployed its new Messerschmitt Bf 109G and Focke Wulf Fw 190A fighters, whose improved performance enabled them to catch the reconnaissance Spitfires. Losses mounted. In reply, the new Rolls-Royce Merlin 61 engine with a two-stage supercharger was introduced into reconnaissance Spitfires, giving greatly improved performance at high altitude. In the spring of 1943 the new variant entered service as the Spitfire XI, able to photograph targets from altitudes around 41,000 feet. These aircraft enjoyed about a year of near-immunity from fighter interception, provided they remained at high altitude. If an aircraft was lost it was usually after it had descended, either to go beneath cloud to take photographs or due to a technical failure.

As the war progressed the RAF reconnaissance force expanded steadily. By May 1942, No. 1 PRU possessed six flights of Spitfires and two of Mosquitoes, with a total of 65 aircraft. That October, No. 1 PRU was re-organised along traditional RAF lines, the Mosquitoes going to No. 540 Squadron and the Spitfires being divided between Nos 541, 542 and 543 Squadrons.

Also during 1942 an important new aerial camera entered service, the F52. For high altitude photography the lens of choice was the 36-in, which produced photographs to a scale of about 1:13,000 from a Spitfire flying at 40,000 feet. That scale was sufficiently small to allow photo interpreters to observe and analyse, for example, the trucks in a

Captured Spitfire PR XI operated by the *Zircus Rosarius*, a unit which toured Luftwaffe bases giving demonstrations of enemy aircraft types. (*Niediee*)

railway siding, the state of construction of a U-boat or the layout of a radar installation.

In August 1943 the US Eighth Air Force established its own photographic reconnaissance unit, the 7th Photo Group, at Mount Farm near Benson. From the start there was close cooperation between RAF and USAAF reconnaissance units, with much interchange of equipment and sharing of knowledge. Initially the 7th Photo Group flew the F-5, the reconnaissance version of the P-38 Lightning fighter. This aircraft was vulnerable to interception during deep penetrations into enemy territory, however, and it had serviceability problems. One squadron in the Group was therefore equipped with Spitfire PR XIs, and operated the type for the rest of the conflict.

The Spitfire XI's period of near-invulnerability to interception lasted until the summer of 1944, and ended with the appearance of the first German jet fighters. Flying alone and unarmed, the reconnaissance Spitfires offered perfect targets for the Messerschmitt 163 and Me 262 pilots to practise their interception techniques. By then, however, the Spitfire PR 19 powered by the Rolls-Royce Griffon engine was on the point of entering service. We shall take a closer look at this aircraft, and some of the reconnaissance operations it later performed, in Chapter 16.

As we have observed in this chapter, the success of the reconnaissance Spitfire had depended to a large extent on the ability to make huge improvements to its range performance. In the next chapter we shall look at the work done in parallel to extend the range of fighter variants of the Spitfire.

Spitfire PR XIs of the 14th Photo Squadron, 7th Photo Group of the US Eighth Air Force, which operated the type from Mount Farm near Oxford.

CHAPTER 7

THE QUEST FOR RANGE

The operations over northern Europe in May and June 1940, culminating in the Dunkirk evacuation, highlighted a major limitation of the Spitfire in that type of combat. Reginald Mitchell had designed it as a short-range interceptor, a role where the most important parameters were high speed, high rate of climb and sufficient firepower to knock down enemy bombers or reconnaissance planes with a few short bursts. An interceptor fighter needed a radius of action only sufficient to reach and engage enemy planes heading to or from targets in friendly territory. For this role the early versions of the Spitfire carried 85 gallons of fuel in two tanks positioned immediately in front of the pilot. That gave the fighter an effective combat radius of action of about 100 miles and, for air defence operations, that was just about adequate.

The first serious attempt to test an option for increasing the range of the Spitfire took place early in 1940. Trials aircraft K9791 was fitted with a mock-up installation of a fixed tank under each wing. Intended to provide extra range for ferry operations, these tanks could not be jettisoned but would be removed before entering combat in the new operational area.

The idea of mounting two fixed tanks under the Spitfire's wings was not taken

Spitfire K9791, repaired after her belly landing in September 1939, pictured early the following year with a mock-up installation of two fixed underwing fuel tanks.

Spitfire I fitted with the trials installation for the fixed 30-gallon tank under the port wing.

further, but in May 1940 trials Spitfire P9565 appeared with a single fixed 30-gallon tank under the port wing. The report on the handling characteristics of the aircraft stated that these were poor at low speed. Moreover, in dives at speeds greater than 350 mph (indicated) 'considerable force' was required on the ailerons to hold up the port wing.

The Mark I with the asymmetric tank arrangement did not enter production. With the Battle of Britain about to begin, the need was for as many standard Spitfires as possible. For the time being the idea of improving the range of the Spitfire had to be put on the back burner.

At the end of 1940, RAF Fighter Command commenced its programme of

offensive sweeps and bomber escort missions over north-west Europe. That re-kindled interest in the long-range version of the fighter, and Supermarine built about sixty Spitfire Mark IIs with a 40-gallon fixed tank under the port wing. Designated the Mark II Long Range, these aircraft first saw action in the spring of 1941.

The new variant was not popular with the pilots. Flight Sergeant Walter Johnson flew this variant with No. 152 Squadron, and he had nothing good to say about it:

That lopsided tank was the worst thing they ever did to the Spitfire, it made the plane a pig to handle. For take-off we had to use full starboard trim, almost full right

Spitfire II Long Range, fitted with the larger 40-gallon tank under the port wing. About sixty examples of this variant were built. (*Lambermont*)

A Spitfire LR II of No. 19 Squadron. During the latter part of the 1941 these aircraft shuffled between squadrons, as units being withdrawn from the south of England passed their long-range Spitfires to the unit that replaced them. (*via Hurt*)

rudder and the stick almost hard over in the same direction. Flying circuits and bumps to get the feel of the plane was a dicey business, because it meant the take-offs *and* the landings were made with an almost full wing tank. We could not use the usual curving approach to keep the ground in sight, not with the extra 250 to 300 pounds of extra weight under the port wing. Instead, we trundled in as if the runway was that of an aircraft carrier. We lost two pilots who under-cooked the final turn and slipped straight in – Bang!

Compared with the standard Mark II the Long Range version was less manoeuvrable: its maximum speed was 26 mph lower, it took nearly 3 minutes longer to reach 20,000 feet and its service ceiling was 3,700 feet lower.

Yet, unpopular though they were, these aircraft were worked hard during the latter half of 1941. At this time Fighter Command rotated Spitfire squadrons through bases in the south of England, so that the entire force could gain combat experience during operations over Europe. As a squadron withdrew to rest and retrain, it passed its Long Range Spitfires to the squadron that replaced it. Thus several units flew the LR Mark II in combat, in some cases for only a short time. Nos 19, 66, 118, 152, 222, 234, 501 and 616 Squadrons all operated this variant.

By the spring of 1942, the formidable Focke Wulf Fw 190 fighter was firmly established at bases in France and Belgium. The new German fighter had a clear edge in performance over the Spitfire V, the best fighter the RAF had at the time. Over the standard Spitfire II the performance margin was even greater, and compared with the Long Range Mark II the margin was greater still. The latter were relegated to operations in areas where they were less likely to encounter the Fw 190, until finally the squadrons were re-equipped with Mark Vs.

The need to increase the range of the Spitfire was obvious, but it was equally clear that the fixed underwing tank was not the answer. To the modern reader the drop tank is the obvious answer to the problem, but in the spring of 1941 no such tank had been developed for the Spitfire.

The driving force to develop a drop tank for the Spitfire came from the need to deliver batches of these fighters to the beleaguered island of Malta. Like the Hurricanes delivered to the island earlier, these would be carried about halfway to the island by aircraft carrier. They would then take off and fly the rest of the way to Malta, a distance of about 660 miles or about as far as from London to Prague. To that end Supermarine engineers designed and built a 90-gallon jettisonable slipper tank to fit under the fuselage of the fighter, which more than doubled the fuel load it could carry. The fighter's fuel system had to be redesigned to enable it to draw fuel from the new tank.

After delivery to Gibraltar by freighter, the modified Spitfires were assembled and lifted by crane on to the deck of the aircraft carrier HMS *Eagle*. Everything was done in a rush as Corporal Ray Honeybone, one of the RAF ground crewmen on the carrier, explained:

Under the fuselage and in line with the mainplanes was a three-point mounting, the centre one of which was retractable so that the tank could be jettisoned. There was also a device consisting of a spring-loaded mushroom valve in the cockpit floor, which mated with a seating on the upper surface of the jettison tank. Mating can be a loose term in engineering but it was necessary to arrange that the tanks stayed securely fixed to the fuselage and at the same time the mushroom valve and seat met in a perfect contact, otherwise fuel did not flow upwards to the carburettor. As each aircraft was brought to the stage where engines could be run, again after dark, each was towed topside on deck and put through its paces. A cock provided selection from Main Fuel to Auxiliary Fuel and it seemed logical to expect that fluid should flow. But almost as soon as the cock was turned, a small red light indicated lack of fuel pressure. And try as we may, it was a hit and miss affair to arrange the tank and valve position to work with much measure of success.

On 27 February 1942, HMS *Eagle* set out from Gibraltar with her precious cargo, escorted by a battle group which included the carrier *Argus*, a battleship, a cruiser and nine destroyers. Still the slipper tanks gave trouble as Flight Lieutenant Stanley Grant, who was to lead the formation of fighters to the island, explained:

The next day, when we were well clear of land, Hughes [Squadron Leader 'Shorty' Hughes, the senior RAF engineering officer] brought the aircraft up on deck to run the engines and, above all, to test the functioning of the long-range tanks without which the operation was not on. These first 90-gallon tanks had evidently been produced in a great hurry and were a bit of a lash-up. The fuel was drawn up into the main tanks by suction and if there was the slightest air leak in the seal between the tank and the fuselage, there was no transfer.

Hughes soon found that the seals were not satisfactory and although he and his team strove hard all that day and well into the night he could not make them work properly. Accordingly, around midnight, with our take-off due the next morning, Hughes sent a message to the Admiral via Wing Commander Maclean [the senior RAF officer], saying that the aircraft could not be allowed to take off without further extensive tests.

When he heard that, the Royal Navy Admiral commanding the operation nearly exploded. He said that under no circumstances could his ships hang around in daylight in the middle of the Mediterranean, within easy range of enemy bombers. He said the Spitfires would have to take off the next morning – at all costs. But Hughes was adamant that the aircraft were not serviceable. He would not agree to let them take off until he was certain that the tanks worked properly, and in most cases they did not. So the Admiral had to give in, and the warships turned around and steamed back to Gibraltar.

Once *Eagle* reached Gibraltar there was hectic activity to get the Spitfires' new fuel tanks to work properly. The Supermarine engineer who designed the jettisonable tank was flown out to assist with the work. When he saw the tanks he immediately pinpointed the reason why so many had failed to work properly. While it was vitally important to establish a good seal between the tank and the fuselage, there was another problem that had not been made clear to those who had fitted the tanks. At the lowest point of each tank was a small bulbous protrusion that acted as a sump, and the fuel transfer pipe reached almost to the bottom of that sump. If that sump was dented it blocked the end of the transfer pipe and so prevented fuel transfer. In the course of fitting them to the aircraft, by people unfamiliar with the new system, several of the tanks had suffered dented sumps. The remedy was to cut away the dented area and solder a patch over the cut-away area. That cured the problem, and after repair the damaged tanks all transferred fuel satisfactorily.

Early on the morning of 5 March HMS *Eagle* and her covering force set sail again. Soon after dawn on 7 March the carrier reached the planned flying-off position off the coast of Algeria, and launched her batch of fifteen Spitfires. All reached Malta safely.

The deck control officer drops his chequered flag and a Spitfire V carrying a 90-gallon drop tank begins the take-off run from aircraft carrier USS *Wasp*, during the Malta reinforcement operation on 19 April 1942. (*US Navy*)

During the months to follow a further 370 Spitfires would be delivered to the island by aircraft carrier.

Following the successful use of the 90-gallon drop tank for the Malta ferry missions, smaller tanks were built to carry 30 gallons and 45 gallons. Intended for use by fighters flying combat missions, these were jettisoned before going into action and were used in very large numbers.

The need to use aircraft carriers to deliver Spitfires to Malta tied down these scarce and valuable ships and prevented their use for other tasks. Accordingly, Supermarine was asked to examine a way of modifying the Spitfire to fly from Gibraltar to Malta in a single hop. That distance, just over 1,100 miles, was about as far as from London to St Petersburg in Russia. For that purpose

Supermarine developed a 170-gallon slipper tank. The aircraft also carried a 29-gallon fuel tank behind the pilot's seat, and an enlarged oil tank in the nose. To save weight all its weapons were removed, except for the two inboard .303-in machine guns. During the final three months of 1942, seventeen Spitfires took off from Gibraltar to fly to Malta in a single hop; all except one did so successfully. Had there been a need the flights could have continued, but by then the siege of the island was lifted and Spitfires could be delivered by conventional means.

During 1944 a new type of 90-gallon drop tank began to appear on Spitfires, shaped like a cigar and giving less drag than its predecessor. Both the slipper and the cigar-shaped tanks continued in use until the end of the war.

A Spitfire V with the bulbous 170-gallon drop tank, a 29-gallon tank in the rear fuselage and an enlarged oil tank in the nose, about to take off from Gibraltar for the 1,100 mile flight to Malta in October 1942. (*RAF Museum*)

A Spitfire IX carrying a 30-gallon slipper tank.

Spitfire IXs of No. 74 Squadron pictured at Schijndel in Holland early in 1945. The unit made frequent incursions of some distance into enemy territory, resulting in a heavy expenditure of drop tanks. In the foreground are a dozen 30-gallon tanks ready for immediate use. (*Murland*)

Late production Spitfires Mark IX (depicted here) and Mark XVI aircraft had two additional fuel tanks fitted in the rear fuselage, with a combined capacity of 72 imp. gallons. In this photograph the upper fuel tank and the filler pipe are visible under the rear cockpit glazing. With the rear tank full, the fighter's longitudinal stability was poor and it was limited to a maximum altitude of 15,000 feet.

During 1944 a new and more streamlined 90-gallon drop tank was introduced for the Spitfire, seen here fitted to a Mark IX of No. 72 Squadron operating over the south of France in August 1944.

CHAPTER 8

TAILORED FOR THE TASK – THE SPITFIRE LF IX

The Spitfire IX was essentially a Mark V fitted with the Merlin 61 engine with a two-stage supercharger. The variant entered service during the early summer of 1942, as a hastily introduced counter to the German Focke Wulf Fw 190 fighter, after the latter had demonstrated a clear superiority in performance over the Spitfire V.

Also during the summer of 1942 the RAF captured an example of the Fw 190A-3 intact, and used it to fly comparative performance tests against a range of Allied fighter types. Considering they were quite different aircraft, built to differing operational concepts, the performances of the early production Spitfire IX and the Fw 190A-3 were remarkably close. The RAF trials report noted:

> At 2,000 ft the Fw 190 is 7–8 mph faster than the Spitfire IX
>
> At 5,000 ft the Fw 190 and the Spitfire IX are approximately the same
>
> At 8,000 ft the Spitfire IX is 8 mph faster than the Fw 190
>
> At 15,000 ft the Spitfire IX is 5 mph faster than the Fw 190
>
> At 18,000 ft the Fw 190 is 3 mph faster than the Spitfire IX
>
> At 21,000 ft the Fw 190 and the Spitfire IX are approximately the same
>
> At 25,000 ft the Spitfire IX is 5–7 mph faster than the Fw 190

Armed with this detailed information on the performance of the Fw 190, Rolls-Royce engineers modified the Merlin to have different supercharger gear ratios and a cropped second impeller designed to give the fighter its maximum speed at a somewhat lower altitude than with the original Merlin 61 engine. But with that change, fitted with the new Merlin 66 engine, the Spitfire IX had an edge in performance over the Fw 190 throughout the full range of altitude bands.

The new variant of the Spitfire entered service in 1943, before an official designation had been allocated to it. Squadron pilots needed to differentiate between Mark IXs fitted with the Merlin 66 and earlier sub-variants powered by Merlin 61 or 63 engines. Accordingly the new sub-variant became known unofficially as the 'Mark IXB'. The earlier Spitfire IXs powered by Merlin 61 or 63 engines then became known unofficially as 'Mark IXAs'. (Some published sources have suggested that the 'A' and 'B' designations referred to the type of armament fitted to the aircraft, but this was not the case.)

In the spring of 1943 fighter ace Wing Commander Alan Deere took command of the Biggin Hill Wing, as that unit received the first Mark IXs powered by Merlin 66 engines. In his book *Nine Lives* Deere described the latest sub-variant of the Spitfire in glowing terms:

> I was now all set to renew my acquaintance with the formidable Focke Wulf, but this time I was better equipped. The Biggin Hill squadrons were using the

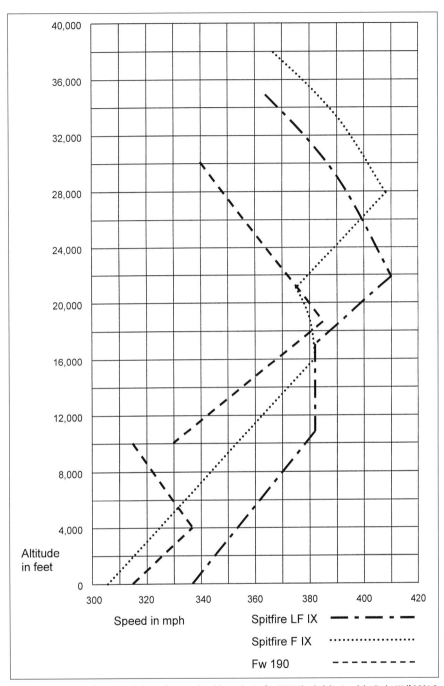

Altitude in feet

Speed in mph

Spitfire LF IX — · — · —

Spitfire F IX ·····················

Fw 190 — — — — — —

This graph shows the performances of the Spitfire F.IX (dotted line), the Spitfire LF.IX (dot-dash line) and the Focke Wulf 190A-3 (dashed line). The original Spitfire IX sub-variant, the F.IX, was superior in performance to the Fw 190 at most altitudes, except below 5,000 feet and between 18,000 and 21,000 feet. The Spitfire LF.IX was designed specifically to eliminate those two areas of advantage for the Fw 190A-3. The new Spitfire was powered by a Merlin 66 engine with a cropped supercharger blower, which allowed the LF.IX to develop its maximum speed at 22,000 feet instead of 28,000 feet in the case of the F.IX. That relatively small change gave the Spitfire LF.IX a clear speed advantage over the Fw 190A-3 at all altitudes.

Externally the Spitfire LF.IX with the Merlin 66 engine looked no different from earlier sub-variants of the Mark IX. To identify individual aircraft it is necessary to consult their record cards. This LF.IX, MH819 of No. 310 (Czech) Squadron, was levelled off prior to gun harmonisation at Appeldram in June 1944. (*Hurt*)

Spitfire IXB (Merlin 66) [author's italics] a mark of Spitfire markedly superior in performance to the FW 190 below 27,000 feet. Unlike the Spitfire IXA, with which all other Spitfire IX Wings in the Group were equipped, the IXB's supercharger came in at a lower altitude and the aircraft attained its best performance at 22,000 feet or at roughly the same altitude as the FW 190. At this height it was approximately 30 mph faster, was better in the climb and vastly more manoeuvrable.

Later in 1943, in a belated attempt to resolve the confusion, the Ministry of Aircraft Production introduced a set of official designations to cover the sub-variants of the Mark IX:

F. IXC (unofficially referred to as the 'Mark IXA'). Aircraft fitted with Merlin 61, 63 or 63A engines, with the C-type wing and armament.

LF IXC (unofficially referred to as the 'Mark IXB'). Aircraft fitted with the Merlin 66 engine and with C-type wing and armament. Although the LF designation implied that this version was optimised for low altitude operations, in fact its high altitude performance was only slightly reduced and the fighter developed its maximum speed at 22,000 feet (compared with 28,000 feet for the F. Mark IX).

Mark V Spitfires of No. 416 and 421 (Canadian) Squadrons with distinctive white-stripe markings. These were worn by one side's fighters during Exercise Spartan in March 1943, when designated units operated under field conditions as part of the preparations for the invasion of northern Europe.

HF IXC. Version fitted with the Merlin 70 engine, with the C-type wing and armament provision. This version was optimised for operations at extreme altitude.

That official edict reached the operational units long after the designations 'Mark IXA' and 'Mark IXB' had become firmly established at the squadrons. As a result, pilots' logbooks and squadron record books would continue to use the unofficial designations throughout the service lives of these variants.

(This page and overleaf top) Spitfire F.VIIs of No. 131 Squadron pictured in the spring of 1944. This version was optimised for high altitude operations, and featured a pressurised cabin. It could also, as shown here, feature the extended span pointed wing tips, though later in the war these were removed and replaced with the normal rounded wing tips. (*Nicholson*)

Spitfire F.IX MA 587 was an interesting hybrid that did not enter production. The aircraft was fitted with a Rotol contra-rotating propeller, Mark XIV-type enlarged tail surfaces and a retractable tail wheel.

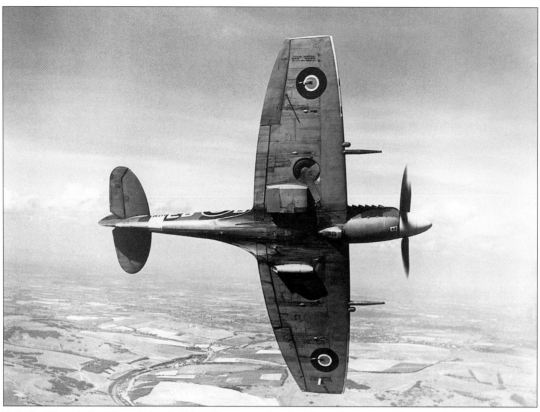

The Spitfire F.XII was the first Griffon-engined version of the Spitfire to enter service, where it formed the equipment of Nos 41 and 91 Squadrons. Optimised for the low altitude combat role, this variant had clipped wings to increase its rate of roll at the expense of high altitude performance.

CHAPTER 9

PRODUCTION FLIGHT TESTING

Throughout 1943 and 1944 Spitfires were coming off the production line at the Castle Bromwich plant at a rate of about three hundred aircraft per month. Each one had to be flight tested before delivery. During his rest tour from operations, Flight Lieutenant Jim Rosser served as a production test pilot. In this chapter he describes the standard procedure for carrying out this important task.

After a thorough pre-flight check, the pilot took off. The first part of the test was to

check and if necessary correct the plane's aileron trim (Spitfire variants prior to the Mark 21 did not have aileron trim tabs):

First I would make a brief 10-minute flight to see if the aircraft could be flown hands off – if it did it was very rare, usually there was a tendency for the Spitfire to lean to one side or the other. Having found which wing dropped, I would land and taxi to one end of the airfield. There a man would be

Senior Test Pilot at Castle Bromwich, Alex Henshaw (second from right) and other pilots preparing for another day's production test flying from the airfield alongside the plant. (*Henshaw*)

New Spitfire LF.IXs on the flight line outside the Castle Bromwich factory, ready for flight testing or delivery to RAF maintenance units which would issue them to squadrons. When this photograph was taken, in May 1944, the forty-three Spitfires shown represented about one week's production at the giant plant. In the background are Lancaster bombers, also being produced at Castle Bromwich. (*Vickers*)

Production of Spitfire XVIs in full swing at Castle Bromwich in 1945. These aircraft have cut-back rear fuselages with teardrop canopies, and clipped wings. (*Vickers*)

waiting with a special tool rather like a tuning fork. I would pull up beside him with the hood open, and beckon him over. I would hold up one, two or three fingers, point to one aileron and point either up or down. He would use his tool to put that number of bends in the required direction in the trailing edge of the metal aileron. Then he would walk to the other aileron and do the same thing in the opposite direction. It was all a bit Heath Robinson, but it worked. Then I would take off again to see if the fighter would fly hands-off. If one wing still dropped I would land immediately to repeat the process, but usually one set of adjustments was sufficient.

Once the aileron trim was OK, I would climb at set revolutions to the fighter's rated altitude, then do a straight and level run at maximum speed. On the squadrons I had flown with, there was always the odd aircraft that seemed to fly faster or slower than the others for a given rpm. Interestingly, if that happened during a production test flight, we were told to get the rev counter changed.

After the maximum speed run I would dive the aircraft to its maximum permitted speed, and see that it handled and recovered in the normal way. If I felt like it I might do some aerobatics, but these were not part of the test programme. All the

things to be found doing aerobatics would have been found out earlier, anyway. Then I would return to the airfield, do a couple of selections of the undercarriage to see that it worked properly, then go in and land. And that was it.

The initial test flight lasted about ten minutes, the second one about thirty minutes. It was laid down that the aircraft had to be test flown for an hour, but in fact it could be proven perfectly well in half an hour.

After landing, the ground staff rectified any faults we had found. Sometimes it was necessary to change an aileron, if the rivets were too close to the edge to allow it to be bent as required. On other occasions the rev counter might need to be changed. Sometimes the undercarriage gave trouble and had to be blown down using the emergency air.

During my time at Castle Bromwich I never found, nor did I hear of any of the other production test pilots finding, an aircraft with dangerous flying characteristics due to poor workmanship. This was remarkable, considering many of the workers had been rapidly trained after coming from jobs that were vastly different – many of the women had been shop assistants, cooks and waitresses, for example.

CHAPTER 10

SPITFIRE MOST SUCCESSFUL

From surviving records it appears probable that EN398, a Mark IX, was the most successful Spitfire of them all in action. She was assembled at Chattis Hill near Andover and came off the production line early in February 1943. She made her maiden flight on the 13th. Five days later she was delivered to RAF Kenley, the home of four Canadian Spitfire units: Nos 403 and 416 Squadrons with Mark IXs, and Nos 411 and 421 Squadrons with Mark Vs.

The Spitfire was in the hangar undergoing acceptance checks when Wing Commander 'Johnnie' Johnson arrived at Kenley to command the Canadian fighter wing. At that time Johnson's personal victory score stood at seven enemy aircraft destroyed plus two shared, four probably destroyed and five damaged. In his autobiography *Wing Leader*, Johnson described his introduction to EN398:

I found the engineer officer and together we had a look at her, gleaming and bright in a new spring coat of camouflage paint. Later I took her up for a few aerobatics to get the feel of her, for this was the first time I had flown a [Spitfire Mark] 9. She seemed very fast, the engine was sweet and she responded to the controls as only a thoroughbred can. I decided that she should be mine, and I never had occasion to regret the choice.

Thus the careers of 'Johnnie' Johnson and Spitfire EN398 became entwined.

Having selected his personal mount, Johnson exercised his Wing Leader's prerogative to have his initials, JEJ, painted on the fuselage in place of the usual squadron code letters. He also had the fighter's weapons re-harmonised to his taste. Before delivery to units, Spitfires had their cannon and machine guns harmonised to a standard pattern that spread the rounds over a circle a few yards across. That gave a pilot of average ability the best chance to score hits. Johnson's shooting skills were far above the average, however, and he ordered that his weapons be set to converge the rounds on a single point ahead of the aircraft, to inflict maximum destruction at that point.

As Johnson became familiar with his new mount, he discovered that she had a small but unusual idiosyncrasy. He commented to the author:

The aeroplane always flew with the turn needle of the turn-and-bank indicator a little bit to one side, even when flying straight and level and on an absolutely even keel. That was disconcerting sometimes when you were flying on instruments, because if you corrected for it you would swing off to one side. Changing the turn-and-bank instrument did not cure it – it must have been something to do with the aeroplane. I even took the aeroplane to Eastleigh and had Jeffrey Quill fly it. I asked if he could have it put right. I left it at the works for a few days but they couldn't cure the problem.

A youthful-looking Wing Commander 'Johnnie' Johnson, pictured beside his personal Spitfire IX, EN398. On either side of the nose the aircraft carried the maple leaf emblem of the Canadian Spitfire Wing that he led. (*RAF Museum*)

Since the Spitfire handled so beautifully in every other respect, the fighter ace decided to live with the small failing.

During the latter part of March, Johnson led his Wing on four separate operations over northern France, flying EN398 each time. And on each occasion, the Spitfire returned without having fired her guns in anger.

It was different on Johnson's next mission, on 3 April. That afternoon his two Mark IX squadrons provided top cover for Typhoons delivering a dive-bombing attack on Abbeville airfield. The raid drew a vigorous German fighter reaction and Johnson was able to manoeuvre his squadrons into a position above and behind a similar number of Focke Wulf 190s. In the 'bounce' that followed, the Spitfires achieved total surprise. Johnson hauled EN398 into a firing position behind one German fighter:

I missed the 190 with my first short burst and steadied the gun platform with coarse stick and rudder. I fired again and hit him on the wing root and just behind the cockpit. The spot harmonisation paid off and the cannon shells thudded into him in a deadly concentration of winking explosions. He started to burn, but before he fell on his back I gave him another long burst. Then I broke away in a steep climbing turn and searched the sky behind. Still nothing there.

During the action the Spitfires claimed five Fw 190s shot down, one probably destroyed and one damaged, for the loss of one of their number.

By the end of June Johnson had added a further eleven victories, and two shared victories, to his score and that of EN398. He was also awarded the Distinguished Service

Order, in recognition of his own rising score and that of the Wing he led so effectively into action.

EN398 was now established as Johnson's personal aircraft. Only he flew her, unless he was absent from the unit for some reason and the Wing needed her to make up the numbers for an operation. That occurred on 20 June when Squadron Leader Robert McNair, commanding No. 421 Squadron, flew EN398 in action and was credited with the destruction of an Fw 190.

After a spell of well-earned leave, Johnson resumed operations on 15 July, when he led the Wing on a fighter sweep and added a Me 109 to his score. His run of successes in EN398 continued with a Me 109 destroyed on the 25th, one damaged on the 29th, a share in the destruction of one more on the 30th, a further share in a Me 109 destroyed, and another of these aircraft damaged on 12 August.

On 17 August the Canadian Wing escorted B-17 Flying Fortresses during the initial part of their penetration to attack the important ball-bearing factories at Schweinfurt. The Spitfires then returned to Kenley to refuel, and took off again to escort the badly mauled raiding force during its withdrawal. The Canadian Wing arrived in time to break up an attack on part of the bomber formation, and Johnson and three other pilots shared in the destruction of a Messerschmitt Bf 110. Five days later Johnson shot down another Me 109.

Since he had made EN398 his personal Spitfire back in March, Johnson had flown the fighter to the exclusion of all others. Near the end of August she needed to go to Air Service Training at Hamble, to receive a replacement engine. While she was there Johnson flew a borrowed Spitfire on the 26th and on 4 September, when he shot down two more Fw 190s.

On 5 September Johnson was again in action in EN398, and was credited with one Messerschmitt Bf 109 damaged. He flew her on operations on the 6th and twice on the 8th, but had no further contact with enemy planes. A few days later he relinquished command of the Wing and was posted to No. 11 Group Headquarters.

During his six month operational tour Johnson had been flying EN398 when he shot down twelve enemy aircraft, shared in the destruction of five more and inflicted damage on a further seven enemy aircraft. In addition Squadron Leader Robert McNair had flown her on 20 June, when he shot down an Fw 190. Thus, adding up the half shares in victories, EN398 can be credited with the destruction of fifteen enemy aircraft and causing damage to seven more. She never had to return early from a mission due to technical failure, and in Johnson's skilful hands she never suffered so much as a scratch in combat.

Having achieved so much, the reader might think that EN398 deserved an honourable retirement in an air museum somewhere. Alas, people did not think that way four years into a hard-fought conflict. As Johnson moved away and took up his staff appointment, life went rapidly downhill for his once-pampered Spitfire.

For a couple of weeks EN398 served with No. 421 Squadron, but then she suffered damage in an unspecified accident and went to Air Service Training Ltd at Hamble for repair. The next mention on her record card was in March 1944, when she arrived at No. 83 Group Support Unit at Redhill to await re-allocation to a unit. By that stage of the war brand new Spitfires arrived at the unit faster than the operational units were asking for replacements. The newest Spitfires to arrive were the first to be allocated, so EN398 went progressively down the queue and she was still at the Support Unit when war in Europe ended.

In May 1945, EN398 was allocated to No. 80 Operational Training Unit at Ouston in Northumberland, where French pilots were being taught to fly the large number of Spitfires bought by that country. While she was at the training unit, EN398 undoubtedly suffered much harsh treatment from novice pilots ignorant of her distinguished past.

In March 1946, No. 80 OTU disbanded. EN398 made her last flight, to No. 29 Maintenance Unit at High Ercal, Shropshire, where she was placed in long-term storage. Her end came suddenly in October 1949 when, without ceremony or remorse, she was sold to H. Bath & Son Ltd and carted off for scrap.

CHAPTER 11

SPITFIRES WITH SEA BOOTS

During the campaign in Norway in April 1940 the RAF suffered greatly from the lack of airfields on which to base its fighters. The Air Staff issued an urgent requirement for the construction of prototypes of floatplane versions of the Spitfire and Hurricane. A Mark I Spitfire, R6722, was passed to Folland Aircraft Ltd at Hamble for the fitting of a set of floats designed for the Blackburn Roc naval fighter.

Although the work progressed rapidly, in Norway events moved even faster. The campaign ended in defeat before the prototype Spitfire floatplane was ready to fly. That ended the requirement for the floatplane fighter. So R6722 had her floats removed and she was returned to the landplane fighter configuration. After that the idea of the Spitfire floatplane lay dormant for a couple of years.

In 1942 the idea of the floatplane fighter idea was revived and Folland Aircraft Ltd converted a Spitfire V, W3760, to that configuration. The fighter was fitted with a pair of floats specially designed for her by Arthur Shirvall at Supermarine, who more than a decade earlier had designed the high speed floats for the Schneider Trophy racing seaplanes. The new floatplane fighter was powered by a Merlin 45 engine driving a four-bladed propeller, and had a fin extension below the rear fuselage to provide additional keel area to compensate for the directional instability caused by the floats. The floatplane carried a spin recovery parachute and a guard to prevent it snagging on the rudder horn balance. On 12 October 1942

Jeffrey Quill flew the Spitfire floatplane for the first time, from Southampton Water.

The initial test flights of W3760 revealed that her directional stability was not good enough, so she was fitted with a revised fin giving increased area. Later she had her armament of two 20 mm cannon and four .303 machine guns installed.

In January 1943 the floatplane went to the Marine Aircraft Experimental Establishment at Helensburgh near Glasgow for its service trials. Fully loaded, the floatplane version of the fighter weighed just over 1,100 lb more than the equivalent landplane version. The maximum speed of the floatplane was 251 mph at sea level, 285 mph at 10,000 feet and 324 mph at 19,500 feet. In each case those speeds were about 40 mph less than the equivalent landplane version, and the rate of climb was about 400 ft/min less throughout the altitude range. The recommended take-off speed was 115 mph and the recommended alighting speed, with flaps down, was 71 mph.

Test pilots reported that handling on the water during taxiing, take-off and alighting was in general good. Due to propeller torque, turns on the water to port were easier than turns to starboard. Similarly, it was more difficult to taxi on a steady course at slow speeds with the wind on the port side than on the starboard side. The aircraft was taxied without difficulty in crosswinds of up to 12 mph, but if the crosswind exceeded 15 mph it was advisable to shut down the engine and tow the aircraft. Beaching and launching, using the standard beaching gear, presented no difficulties.

The first Spitfire floatplane to fly, Mark V W3760. Note the four-bladed propeller, the lack of a filter on the carburettor air intake, and the original fin arrangement with a small extension on the underside to give increased keel area.

For the take-off, the trials report advised the use of one-third to one-half rudder to correct the swing to port. It went on:

On opening the throttle the control column should be held central. The nose rises at first and then falls as the speed increases. When on the step the control column should be eased back to overcome a slight tendency to nose down further. This tendency is by no means pronounced, and any correction made on the control column should be only slight because the elevator control is light and sensitive. A slight pull on the control column is required for take-off at a speed of 81 to 83 mph IAS [indicated airspeed] in moderate or calm sea conditions.

Once in the air the Spitfire floatplane handled well, apart from developing an appreciable change of elevator trim during dives. For a floatplane the aircraft was considered very manoeuvrable. She stalled at 69 mph with flaps down, and 82 mph with flaps up. In both conditions the stall occurred with the control column almost central with the nose rather high, and there was no increased load on the stick. At the stall there was a fluttering noise and the port wing dropped 20 or 30 degrees. Except for the nose-up attitude, there was no preliminary warning of the stall. Recovery was achieved by easing the control column forward. The floatplane was spun in either direction and the report noted that spinning characteristics were similar to those on the landplane, and were considered satisfactory.

On the approach for alighting on the water, it was recommended that the flaps be lowered at about 1,000 ft at a speed not exceeding 140 mph. When the flaps were lowered, the nose dropped sharply. The best speed for approach was 115 mph, which gave a good forward view and enabled the pilot to judge his height

better than when approaching at a slower speed with more engine. The report then struck a cautionary note:

Care should be exercised during an approach over hangars, trees, etc., because the rate of descent with the engine throttled back is about 2,000 ft/min, a fact which is not apparent at first since the gliding attitude of the aircraft is rather flat.

The test pilots found the best speed for alighting was about 70 mph, with the tail slightly down.

In the summer of 1943, the RAF began detailed planning for an operation to exploit the Spitfire floatplane's unique capability. At that time German garrisons on the Dodecanese Islands in the eastern Mediterranean were dependent on supplies brought in by transport planes. An ambitious plan was hatched to operate Spitfire floatplanes from a concealed base beside an unoccupied island in the chain, to disrupt this important aerial traffic. A submarine would support the operation, carrying the necessary supplies and the ground crew. Between flights the Spitfire floatplanes would sit at their moorings under camouflage. It was the sort of operation that would succeed for only a few days, until the element of surprise was lost and enemy forces moved into the area to hunt for the perpetrators. But while they were in action the floatplane fighters might cause mayhem among the poorly armed transport planes.

Folland Aircraft Ltd received a contract to convert two further Spitfire Vs to the floatplane configuration. In August the work on these aircraft, EP751 and EP754, was completed. After flight testing the new floatplanes, together with W3670, were dismantled and crated. They were then loaded on a freighter and arrived at the port of Alexandria, Egypt, at the end of October.

Jeffrey Quill pictured in the cockpit of W3760.

W3760 taking off from Southampton Water, *c.* October 1942.

After offloading, the three floatplane fighters were transported to the seaplane base at Fanara on the Great Bitter Lake for reassembly. There it was discovered that W3760 had serious corrosion around the tail area. She was put to one side pending the arrival of a replacement tail unit from Folland. The assembly of the two other floatplanes went ahead rapidly, and by the end of November both were ready for flight testing.

At the time, Flight Lieutenant Willie Lindsay was on a 'rest' tour at the Middle East Gunnery School at El Ballah in Egypt. Sitting in his tent one day, he heard a Tannoy announcement asking Spitfire pilots to call at the Adjutant's office and give the number of hours flown on the type. That sounded as if it might produce something interesting, so Lindsay complied. The next thing he knew he was ordered to report to the Station Commander, Wing Commander Wilson MacDonald. The young pilot recalled:

My answers to some prepared questions seemed to satisfy the CO, who then said, 'Lindsay, at this stage I am unable to tell you much about the operation you have volunteered for but it will involve flying seaplanes. Pack your shaving gear and a clean shirt and organise a Harvard for after lunch tomorrow when you will fly me to 107 Maintenance Unit at Kasfareet on the Great Bitter Lake.' I was not aware that I had volunteered for anything, but the prospect of something new and different sounded interesting, and seaplanes at that!

From Kasfareet we drove to the pre-war seaplane base at Fanara and there on the hard standing above the slipway stood two Mk V Spitfires fitted with floats. It was a wonderful moment, I can still feel the tingle of hairs standing up on the back of my neck. With their huge floats, they looked much larger than the normal Spitfire. Back came the thrilling childhood memories of the Schneider Trophy races, the names of Stainforth, Orlebar, Waghorn and others who flew those world-beating Supermarine seaplanes and here I was going to fly a descendant – powerful stuff for a 22-year-old.

Moored beside the slipway was a Walrus biplane flying boat, on which the four selected Spitfire pilots were to learn the rudiments of operating from water. On 30 November each pilot had a brief period of dual instruction on the Walrus, followed by a solo flight on the type. On 2 December, the great day arrived for the pilots to begin conversion training on the Spitfire floatplane. In the mean time, Willie Lindsay had learned that he had been chosen to command the flight of Spitfire floatplanes. That meant he was first to take off in one from the Great Bitter Lake. He continued:

I will admit to being somewhat apprehensive at the pre-flight briefing. It was short and to the point. Standing in the launch and reading from a slip of paper, the CO stressed that I must be prepared for swing at take-off. Gliding and landing speeds were approximately the same but better allow an extra 10 mph or so just to be on the safe side. Lastly and very important, a three-point attitude when alighting so that the extreme end of the floats touched the water first. I recall the CO's words as I climbed onto the float: 'Off you go, Lindsay, be a good lad and don't bend it!'

Once in the floatplane with the engine running, Lindsay opened the throttle halfway to get some idea of the swing he could expect on the take-off run. He found the swing was less than expected, though he was surprised at the long run needed for a take-off. Once

Flight Lieutenant Willie Lindsay was serving at the Middle East Gunnery School at El Ballah in Egypt, when he 'volunteered' to fly the Spitfire floatplane. Had the planned operation in the Aegean taken place, he would have commanded the floatplane flight when it went into action. (*Lindsay*)

The two airworthy floatplanes in Egypt, EP751 and EP754, on the hard standing at Fanara on the Great Bitter Lake. (*via Sissons*)

airborne, he took the floatplane up to 5,000 feet to test her handling. He throttled back and lowered the flaps and found that the plane reacted in the normal way, though with possibly a little more 'dip' than usual. Then, like the test pilots at Helensburgh, he discovered the floatplane's disconcertingly rapid rate of sink in that configuration.

Continuing to glide with the flaps down I lost 500 feet rather faster than I expected or liked; mentally I added another 10 mph to my approach speed. By this time what little breeze there had been at take-off had disappeared and the lake was like a mirror. Fortunately our very experienced Flight Sergeant Cox'n could see that there might

Spitfire floatplane drawn up on the beach at Fanara, between flights. (*via Sissons*)

be a problem for an inexperienced pilot judging height above the surface of the water. Both launches were dispatched to zigzag and roughen the surface, which was helpful. After levelling off there was some additional 'float' due to the increased speed at approach – however, the touch-down was smooth. Speed reduced quickly

on the water with some slight porpoising from the following wave, altogether a pleasant first alighting.

Not surprisingly I found the handling sluggish compared with the land version. On 6 December, before doing a cannon test, I took EP754 to 15,000 feet to test handling at speed and to try some

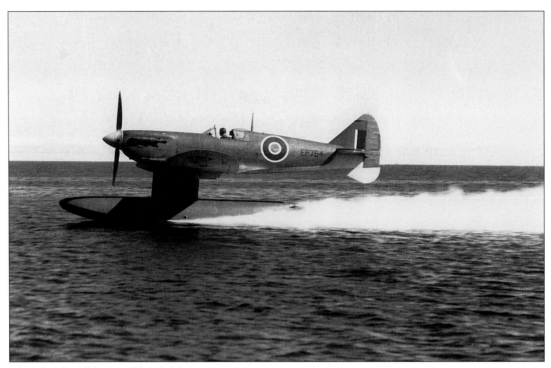

Willie Lindsay taking off during one of the early flights in EP754. (*via Sissons*)

aerobatics. Starting a slow roll at around 240 mph, the roll was more like a barrel roll and the 'barrel' was a big one; at least I was far enough away from critical eyes not to be embarrassed. The loop was better.

I judged it likely that at some stage I would be engaged by enemy fighters and did some further aerobatics and some very tight turns to get the feel of this unusual aircraft. However, I drew the line at test spinning. If I was unfortunate enough to get into that situation, then recovery would probably be via a quick prayer.

All four pilots practised take-offs and alightings, conducting the floatplane version of circuits and bumps. They found no major problems, apart from difficulties in manoeuvring on the water when there was a crosswind.

Soon after his first flight in the floatplane, Willie Lindsay learned the basic details of the operation for which he and the other pilots were preparing. During their flights from the Great Bitter Lake, the pilots found a couple of problems that might jeopardise such a venture. The first was that the Spitfires' floats suffered from small leaks. During operations off the Lake that did not matter, because after each day's flying the aircraft were hauled onto a hard standing and their floats were drained. At a concealed base in a war zone, however, the problem might have been more serious. Another difficulty concerned the difficulty of manoeuvring the floatplanes on the water in crosswinds stronger than 15 mph. During the flights off the Lake, the solution had been to switch off the engine and have a launch tow the floatplane back to the slipway. Again, in a war zone that might have not have been so easy.

Willie Lindsay leading the two serviceable Spitfire floatplanes in formation over Fanara.

In the event, the scheme to send Spitfire floatplanes into action over the Greek islands came to nothing. In October 1943, while the floatplanes were still en route to Egypt, German forces with powerful Luftwaffe backing had re-entered the Dodecanese in strength and ejected British forces from the islands of Kos and Leros. With German fighters now operating in the area in numbers, the plan to operate Spitfire floatplanes in that area was no longer feasible. On 13 December, Lindsay was informed that the operation had been cancelled and he and the other pilots were to return to their units. No other operational use was envisaged for the Mark V float-planes, and they went into storage.

That was not quite the end of the Spitfire floatplane story, however. In the spring of 1944, there were thoughts of using a floatplane version of the Spitfire IX for an operation planned for the Pacific theatre. MJ982 was selected as prototype and underwent conversion in Folland's experimental workshop. The aircraft was then transported to the Saunders-Roe works at Beaumaris on Anglesey for reassembly. Jeffrey Quill took the new variant up for her maiden flight on 18 June 1944. Later he told this writer:

The Spitfire IX on floats was faster than the standard Hurricane. Its handling on the water was extremely good and its only unusual feature was a tendency to tramp from side to side on the floats, or to waddle a bit when at high speed in the plane.

A Spitfire floatplane making a low altitude pass, before alighting on the lake. (*via Sissons*)

Soon after the MJ892 began flying, the scheme to use these aircraft in action was also dropped. The Mark IX floatplane also went into storage, and eventually she and the three Mark V floatplanes were scrapped.

Altogether five Spitfires were converted into floatplanes, and four of them flew. Although none of these aircraft saw action, it is yet another aspect of the story which illustrates again the enormous versatility of Reginald Mitchell's original design.

The Spitfire IX floatplane MJ 892 made her maiden flight in June 1944, and an operation was planned to employ a dozen of these aircraft in the Pacific theatre. The operation was cancelled, however, and after a few flights the Mark IX floatplane was placed in storage. (*Vickers*)

CHAPTER 12

SPITFIRE DEPLOYMENT AT ITS GREATEST EXTENT

This chapter lists the front-line units operating Spitfires at the beginning of June 1944, shortly before the Normandy invasion when the type's deployment stood at about its greatest extent.

With each unit is given the Mark number it operated, and its airfield. Asterisked units (*) also operated other types. Unless otherwise stated, units operated in the fighter role.

Air Defence of Great Britain

No. 10 Group

Nos 1, 165 Sqns	Mark IX	Predannack
No. 41 Sqn	Mark XII	Bolt Head
No. 126 Sqn	Mark IX	Culmhead
Nos 131, 616 Sqns	Mark VII	Culmhead
No. 610 Sqn	Mark XIV	Harrowbeer

No. 11 Group

Nos 33, 74, 127 Sqns	Mark IX	Lympne
Nos 64, 234, 611 Sqns	Mark V	Deanland
Nos 80, 229, 274 Sqns	Mark IX	Detling
Nos 130, 303, 402 Sqns	Mark V	Horne
No. 345 Sqn	Mark V	Shoreham
No. 350 Sqn	Mark V	Friston
No. 501 Sqn	Mark IX	Friston

No. 12 Group

No. 504 Sqn	Mark V	Castletown, Digby, Acklington

No. 13 Group

No. 118 Sqn	Mark V	Skeabrae, Sumburgh

Second Tactical Air Force

No. 83 Group (Mark IXs operated as fighters and fighter-bombers)

No. 125 Wing (Nos 132, 453, 602 Sqns)	Mark IX	Ford
No. 144 Wing (Nos 441, 442, 443 Sqns)	Mark IX	Ford
No. 126 Wing (Nos 401, 411, 412 Sqns)	Mark IX	Tangmere
No. 127 Wing (Nos 403, 416, 421 Sqns)	Mark IX	Tangmere
No. 400 Sqn	Mark XI	Odiham (Photographic Reconnaissance)

Spitfire PR XI of No. 541 Squadron with black and white invasion stripes on the fuselage and wings.

No. 84 Group (Mark IXs operated as fighters and fighter-bombers)
No. 131 Wing (Nos 302, 308, 317 Sqns)	Mark IX	Chailey
No. 132 Wing (Nos 66, 331, 332 Sqns)	Mark IX	Bognor
No. 134 Wing (Nos 310, 312, 313 Sqns)	Mark IX	Appeldram
No. 135 Wing (Nos 222, 349, 485 Sqns)	Mark IX	Selsey
No. 145 Wing (Nos 329, 340, 341 Sqns)	Mark IX	Merston
No. 4 Sqn	Mark XI	Gatwick (PR)

No. 85 Group (Mark IXs operated as fighters and fighter-bombers)

No. 56 Sqn	Mark IX	Newchurch
No. 91 Sqn	Mark XIV	West Malling
No. 124 Sqn	Mark VII	Bradwell Bay
No. 322 Sqn	Mark XIV	Hartford Bridge Flats

Air Spotting Pool

No. 26 Sqn	Mark V	Lee on Solent (Gun Spotting)
No. 63 Sqn	Mark V	Lee on Solent (GS)

Other 2nd Tactical Air Force Units

No. 16 Sqn	Mark IX, XI	Northolt (Tac. Recce)
No. 1401 Flight	Mark IX	Manston (Met. Recce)

Coastal Command

No. 275 Sqn	Mark V	Warmwell* (Search, Rescue)
No. 276 Sqn	Mark V	Portreath* (SAR)
No. 277 Sqn	Mark V	Shoreham* (SAR)
No. 278 Sqn	Mark V	Bradwell Bay* (SAR)
No. 519 Sqn	Mark VI	Wick* (MetR)
No. 1402 Flight	Mark VI	Aldergrove (MetR)
No. 541 Sqn	Marks X, XI	Benson (PR)
No. 542 Sqn	Marks X, XI, 19	Benson (PR)

Army Co-operation Units

No. 288 Sqn	Mark V	Collyweston*

US Eighth Air Force

7th Photo Group	Mark XI	Mount Farm*

Mediterranean Air Command

Italy

Nos 32, 253 Sqns	Mark IX	Foggia
Nos 73, 87 Sqns	Mark V, IX	Foggia
No. 43 Sqn	Mark IX	Nettuno
Nos 72, 111 Sqns	Mark IX	Largo
No. 145 Sqn	Mark VIII	Lago
No. 40 SAAF, 225 Sqns	Mark V, IX	Lago (TacR)
Nos 92, 417, 601 Sqns	Mark VIII	Venafro
No. 208 Sqn	Mark IX	Venafro (TacR)
No. 93 Sqn	Mark IX	Tre Canelli
Nos 249, 1435 Sqns	Mark IX	Grottaglie
No. 241 Sqn	Mark IX	Trigno (TacR)
No. 318 Sqn	Mark V	Trigno (TacR)
Nos 682, 683 Sqns	Mark XI	San Severo (PR)

No. 7 SAAF Fighter Wing

Nos 1, 2, 4, 7 Sqns SAAF	Marks V, IX	Based in Italy

Corsica

Nos 154, 232, 242, 243 Sqns	Mark IX	Poretta
Nos 237, 238, 451 Sqns	Mark IX	Serragia
No. 328 Sqn	Mark IX	Borgo

Malta

No. 185 Sqn	Mark IX	Hal Far

Middle East Command

Libya

No. 94 Sqn	Mark IX	Bu Amud
No. 335 Sqn	Mark V	Bersis

Egypt

No. 213 Sqn	Mark IX	Idku
No. 336 Sqn	Mark IX	Mersa Matruh
No. 680 Sqn	Mark XI	Matariya (PR)

Aden

No. 3 Sqn SAAF	Mark V	Khormaksar

Air Command, South-East Asia

No. 222 Group (Ceylon)

No. 17 Sqn	Mark VIII	Vavuyina
No. 273 Sqn	Mark VIII	Ratmalana

Eastern Air Command (India)

Nos 67, 155 Sqns	Mark VIII	Baigachi

Photographic Reconnaissance Force (India)

No. 681 Sqn*	Mark XI	Alipore (PR)

No. 221 Group (India)

No. 81 Sqn	Mark VIII	Khumbirgram
No. 607 Sqn	Mark VIII	Imphal
No. 615 Sqn	Mark VIII	Palel

No. 224 Group (India)

No. 152 Sqn	Mark VIII	Palel
No. 136 Sqn	Mark VIII	Chittagong

No. 1 Fighter Wing (Australia)

Nos 54, 452, 457 Sqns	Mark VIII	Darwin area

CHAPTER 13

THE NEXT GENERATION: VAMPIRE VERSUS SPITFIRE XIV

During the late 1930s, aircraft designers came to realise that the laws of physics would impose a finite limit to the maximum speed that a propeller-driven plane could attain, and that was somewhere around 500 mph. The problem centred on the propeller's weakness as a means of converting the piston engine's rotational power into thrust. As a plane's speed neared 500 mph, propeller efficiency fell sharply.

A few figures will serve to illustrate the point. In round terms, the Spitfire I attained a maximum speed of about 300 mph at sea level with an engine developing about 1,000 hp. At that speed, propeller efficiency was

The Spitfire F.XIV was one of the fastest variants of this aircraft. In terms of combat performance, however, it was thoroughly outclassed by first-generation jet fighters like the Vampire. (*Vickers*)

about 80 per cent, and the 1,000 lb of thrust it produced equalled the drag from the fighter's airframe.

Now consider the engine power needed to propel the Spitfire I at twice that speed, 600 mph. Drag rises with the square of the speed, thus if the speed is doubled the drag is quadrupled. So 1,000 lb of drag at 300 mph becomes 4,000 lb of drag at 600 mph. To overcome that amount of drag the aircraft needed 4,000 lb of thrust. But at 600 mph the efficiency of the propeller fell to just over 50 per cent, so to drive the aircraft at that speed a piston engine would need to develop about 12,000 hp. In 1945 the best piston engines produced a fraction over one hp for each pound of weight. Thus a piston engine developing the power to propel our notional fighter at 600 mph would weigh about 11,000 lb – nearly double the weight of a Spitfire I.

For high speed flight the turbojet was a fundamentally more efficient type of power unit. It produced its output directly in the form of thrust, with no conversion losses from a propeller. The Goblin turbojet fitted to the de Havilland Vampire F.1 developed 3,100 lb of thrust for a weight of about 1,550 lb, and gave the fighter a maximum level speed of 540 mph at 17,500 feet. No piston engine and propeller combination offered a thrust-to-weight ratio to compare with that, and it was clear that for use in high performance aircraft their days were numbered.

The Mark XIV was one of the fastest variants of the Spitfire, and at the end of the Second World War it was acknowledged to be among the most effective air superiority fighters in service anywhere. Yet in almost every significant aspect of air combat it was outclassed by the Vampire. The comparative trial between the two aircraft took place at the Central Fighter Establishment at West Raynham in the summer of 1946. The report on that trial, excerpts from which are reproduced below, illustrates the clear margin of superiority achieved by the first-generation of jet fighters.

* * *

In making a comparison between the Vampire and Spitfire XIV, the properties of their engines must be realised. The piston engine maintains power throughout the speed range, while the jet engine produces maximum power only at the fighter's maximum speed. Thus the Spitfire had an inherent advantage over a jet aircraft when operating at the lower end of its speed range. The Spitfire XIV used in the trial was a fully operational aircraft fitted with a Griffon 65, giving 2,015 hp at 7,500 ft.

MAXIMUM LEVEL SPEEDS
The Vampire is greatly superior in speed to the Spitfire XIV at all heights, as shown below:

Altitude (ft)	Approx. speed advantage (mph) over Spitfire XIV
0	130
5,000	110
10,000	100
15,000	100
20,000	95
25,000	75
30,000	70
35,000	70
40,000	90

ACCELERATION AND DECELERATION
With both aircraft in line-abreast formation at a speed of 200 mph (indicated), on the word 'Go' both engines were opened up to a maximum power simultaneously. The Spitfire initially drew ahead, but after a period of approximately 25 seconds the Vampire gradually caught up and quickly accelerated past the Spitfire.

The de Havilland Vampire I jet fighter entered service just too late to see action during the Second World War. (*RAF Museum, Charles Brown*)

The rate of deceleration for the Spitfire is faster than the Vampire even when the Vampire uses its dive brakes. Once again this shows that the Vampire's dive brakes are not as effective as they should be.

DIVE

The two aircraft were put into a 40 degree dive in line-abreast formation with set throttles at a speed of 250 mph (indicated). The Vampire rapidly drew ahead and kept gaining on the Spitfire.

ZOOM CLIMB

The Vampire and Spitfire XIV in line-abreast formation were put into a 45 degree dive. When a speed of 400 mph (indicated) had been reached, a zoom climb at fixed throttle settings was carried out at approximately 50 degrees. The Vampire showed itself vastly superior and reached a height 1,000 feet in excess of the altitude of the Spitfire in a few seconds, and quickly increased its lead as the zoom climb continued. The same procedure was carried out at full throttle settings and the Vampire's advantage was outstandingly marked.

CLIMB

The Spitfire XIV climbs approximately 1,000 feet per minute faster than the Vampire up to 20,000 feet.

TURNING CIRCLES

The Vampire is superior to the Spitfire XIV at all heights. The two aircraft were flown in line-astern formation. The Spitfire was positioned on the Vampire's tail. Both aircraft tightened up to the minimum turning circle with maximum power. It became apparent that the Vampire was just able to keep inside the Spitfire's turning circles. After four or five turns the Vampire was able to position itself on the Spitfire's tail so that a deflection shot was possible. The wing loading of the Vampire is 33.1 lb per sq. ft. compared with the Spitfire XIV's 35.1 lb per sq. ft.

RATES OF ROLL

The Spitfire XIV has a faster rate of roll at all speeds. The higher the speed the faster the Spitfire rolls in comparison with the Vampire. As previously mentioned, at speeds of 500 mph (indicated) there is a feeling of overbalance and aileron snatch when attempting to roll the Vampire.

COMBAT MANOEUVRABILITY

The Vampire will out-manoeuvre the Spitfire type of aircraft at all heights, except for initial acceleration at low speeds and in rolling. Due to the Vampire's much higher speed (i.e. 105 mph faster at 20,000 feet) and superior zoom climb, the Spitfire can gain no advantage by using its superior rate of climb in combat.

(Above and opposite) Near the war's end No. 74 Squadron in Holland experimented with fitting a pair of 60-lb air-to-ground rockets under the wings of its Spitfires, carried in addition to a 500-lb bomb under the fuselage. Due to their differing trajectories, however, the rockets and bombs had to be delivered in separate attacks. Of the two weapons, the pilots thought bombs the more effective, and the rockets saw relatively little use. (*Murland*)

A late production Spitfire FR.XIV fitted with a bubble canopy, belonging to No. 268 Squadron. This tactical reconnaissance unit converted to Spitfires during the final month of the war in Europe, and operated it from Twente in Holland. (*Houston*)

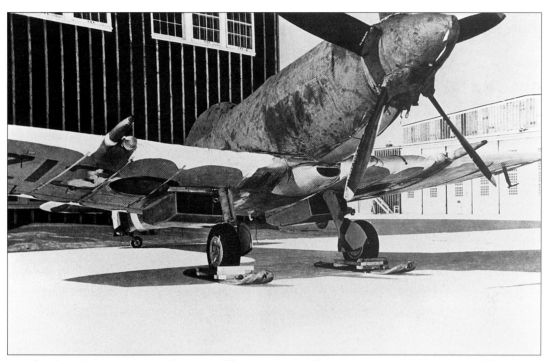

Makeshift skis fitted to Spitfire F.XIV TZ138, to enable her to take off from the snowbound airfield at Le Pas, Manitoba, in 1947. The skis had originally been designed for the Tiger Moth, but they functioned just long enough for the Spitfire to get into the air. Once the fighter was airborne, the skis fell clear. (*via Peter Arnold*)

(This page and opposite) The Spitfire F.21 formed the equipment of No. 41 Squadron based at Lubeck, part of the British occupation force in Germany in 1946. (*Adamson*)

A few Spitfire F.21s were delivered to the RAF fitted with contra-rotating propellers, which greatly improved its stability as a gun platform. The installation did not become general, however.

A Spitfire 21, showing the revised wing shape that distinguished this and later versions of the aircraft.

CHAPTER 14

THE LONGEST SPITFIRE FLIGHT

The immediate postwar period saw an interesting culmination of the wartime work to squeeze as much fuel as possible into, and as much range as possible out of, the Spitfire. James Storey was born in Argentina to Scottish parents, and joined the RAF in 1938. During the war he served with Nos 542 and 543 Squadrons and flew numerous photographic reconnaissance missions in Spitfires. He left the RAF in 1945 and returned to Argentina, where he saw an opportunity to make use of his wartime experiences: to form a company to conduct aerial survey work under contract to the Argentine government.

In 1947 Storey purchased Spitfire XI PL972, together with the necessary photographic equipment and spare parts, from the Air Disposal Section of the Ministry of Supply. Storey decided to fly the Spitfire to Argentina. The longest leg of the planned journey, that from Dakar in Senegal to Natal in Brazil, was 1,850 miles. To cover that distance the Spitfire would carry the normal internal load of 217 imp. gallons, plus a 170 gallon slipper tank, plus two additional 20 gallon tanks in the wings. That gave the aircraft a total fuel capacity of 427 gallons, the largest amount ever carried by a Spitfire. James Storey took charge of the Spitfire, painted in PRU blue and bearing the Argentine registration LV-NMZ, in mid-April 1947.

After a couple of weeks of detailed preparations, Storey took off from Hurn for Gibraltar on 29 April. With a full load of fuel the aircraft weighed 9,700 lb at take-off, which restricted her to straight-and-level flight with gentle manoeuvres until most of the fuel in the slipper tank had been burned.

The initial leg was flown without incident, but that could not be said for the second one flown on the next day. From Gibraltar the Spitfire was to have flown to Senegal, a distance of 1,680 miles. The aircraft encountered strong head winds and a thick sand haze. Storey became lost and was forced to put her down in the desert near Port Etienne in Mauritania (now Nouadhibou) some 400 miles short of his intended destination. With the help of local civilians and a tractor, the Spitfire was dragged to a nearby road where her tanks were filled with sufficient fuel to complete the flight to Dakar the next day.

The Dakar to Natal flight, across the South Atlantic, began during the early morning darkness of 3 May. For this flight Storey was lucky to be able to tag along behind an Avro York airliner of British South American Airways, which was flying on that route on a scheduled service. The pair covered the 1,850 miles to Natal in just over eight hours, with no serious hiccups. On the following day Storey flew the Spitfire from Natal to Rio de Janeiro, and on 5 May he arrived at Moron near Buenos Aires to complete the journey.

Storey arrived just in time to hear bad news: the hoped-for aerial survey contract from the Argentine government was no longer on offer. For most of the year that followed the Spitfire remained on the ground until, in July 1948, Storey sold her to the Argentine Air Force. The latter service operated the Spitfire until 1951, when she suffered damage in a forced landing. Damaged beyond economical repair, the plane was scrapped.

The Spitfire PR XI bearing the Argentine civilian registration LV-NMZ, which James Storey flew in stages from Eastleigh to Buenos Aires in 1947. The leg from Dakar in Senegal to Natal in Brazil, on 3 May, was 1,850 miles and took just over eight hours. It was the longest distance ever flown in a single hop by a Spitfire.

CHAPTER 15

DEPLOYMENT OF RAF SPITFIRE UNITS

JANUARY 1950

By January 1950, jet fighters had replaced the Spitfire in nearly all regular home defence fighter squadrons, though the type continued to serve in large numbers with the Royal Auxiliary Air Force (squadrons numbered in the 500 and the 600 series) and in overseas commands. Except where stated, units operated in the fighter role.

Fighter Command

No. 11 Group

No. 600 Sqn	Mark 21, 22	Biggin Hill
No. 604 Sqn	Mark XVI	North Weald
No. 614 Sqn	Mark 22	Llandow
No. 615 Sqn	Mark 21, 22	Biggin Hill

No. 12 Group

No. 34 Sqn	Mark XVI	Horsham St Faith (Army Co-operation)
No. 502 Sqn	Mark 22	Aldergrove
No. 504 Sqn	Mark 22	Wymeswold
No. 602 Sqn	Mark 22	Abbotsinch
No. 603 Sqn	Mark 22	Turnhouse
No. 607 Sqn	Mark 22	Ouston
No. 608 Sqn	Mark 22	Thornaby
No. 609 Sqn	Mark XVI	Yeadon
No. 610 Sqn	Mark 22	Hooton Park
No. 611 Sqn	Mark 22	Woodvale
No. 612 Sqn	Mark XIV, XVI	Dyce
No. 613 Sqn	Mark 22	Ringway

Coastal Command

Central Photographic Establishment

No. 541 Sqn	Mark 19	Benson (Photographic Recce)

British Air Force of Occupation (Germany)

No. 2 Sqn	Mark XIV	Wunstorf (Fighter Recce)

A Spitfire FR.18 of No. 208 Squadron based at Fayid in the Suez Canal zone in 1950.

Middle East Air Force (Egypt)
    No. 208 Sqn   Mark 18   Fayid (FR)

Far East Air Force
                    Air Headquarters Hong Kong
    No. 28 Sqn   Mark 18   Kai Tak (FR)
    No. 80 Sqn   Mark 24   Kai Tak

                    Air Headquarters Malaya
    No. 60 Sqn   Mark 18   Kuala Lumpur (FR)
    No. 81 Sqn   Mark 19   Tengah (PR)

Spitfire F.24 of No. 80 Squadron based at Kai Tak, Hong Kong, in 1950.

Spitfire F.22s of No. 613 (City of Manchester) Squadron based at Ringway.

During the late 1940s and early 1950s, Spitfires equipped the bulk of the Royal Auxiliary Air Force. This Mark 22 belonged to No. 607 (County of Durham) Squadron based at Ouston. The number 4 painted on the fuselage, wing and tail was the racing number applied to this aircraft for the Cooper Trophy race in 1948.

Intimidating head-on shot of a Spitfire F.22, taken by the famous aviation photographer Charles Brown. (*RAF Museum, Charles Brown*)

CHAPTER 16

COLD WAR WARRIOR

The PR 19 was the final photographic reconnaissance variant of the Spitfire, combining the extra wing tankage and camera installation of the Mark XI with the Griffon engine that powered the Mark XIV fighter. That resulted in a truly outstanding reconnaissance aircraft for its time, with a maximum speed of 445 mph at 26,000 feet and a service ceiling of 42,600 feet. The Spitfire 19 entered service in the summer of 1944. After the initial batch of 25 production aircraft, Mark 19s were fitted with a pressurised cabin, which allowed a pilot to fly in relative comfort while spending long periods at extreme altitude.

The superb altitude performance of the Mark 19 put it beyond the effective engagement reach of the German jet fighters, and by

Fine air-to-air shot of a Spitfire PR 19 in standard PRU blue high altitude camouflage.

the end of the Second World War this variant had replaced the Spitfire XI in most Europe-based strategic reconnaissance squadrons.

If the situation demanded, the Mark 19 could reach altitudes well above its service ceiling. In the RAF that term was defined as the point where the aircraft's rate of climb fell below 100 feet per minute. The figure gave no indication of the height an aircraft could attain if it continued climbing at less than 100 feet per minute, however. During postwar air defence exercises over the United Kingdom, Spitfire 19s running in to photograph targets sometimes clawed their way above 49,000 feet to avoid jet-powered interceptors.

By then the Cold War in the Far East was hotting up, and reconnaissance Spitfires became involved in clandestine photographic missions that have remained secret until recently.

In November 1950 Flight Lieutenant Ted Powles was posted to No. 81 Squadron at Seletar, Singapore, flying Spitfire PR 19s. While with that unit he flew several medium-level photographic reconnaissance flights over Malaya, as part of the campaign against Communist insurgents there. In January 1951 he took command of the Squadron's detached Flight at Kai Tak, Hong Kong, with two PR 19s. Powles soon learned that there was a highly secret aspect to the detachment's work:

A couple of weeks after my arrival at Kai Tak a photographic interpreter came into my office. He laid a map on my desk and asked if I could take aerial photographs of some of the Chinese islands in the local area. There was no mention of any written authorisation to fly over China, though I presumed this had been authorised by higher authority. I told him I would be happy to oblige – as I understood it, that was what I was there to do.

Such a task could not be taken on lightly, however. By then, the Korean War was in full swing and there was a high degree of political tension throughout the area. Moreover, the MiG 15 swept-wing jet fighter had made its appearance over Korea, operating from bases in China close to the border with that country. Although these modern fighters had not yet appeared at airfields nearer to Hong Kong, there could be no certainty that this would remain the case for much longer.

The two Spitfire 19s at Kai Tak, PS852 and PS854, carried split pairs of F52 cameras with 36-in lenses. On 16 January the weather was suitable and Powles took PS852 on his first photographic mission over Chinese territory. By the end of the month he had completed three more reconnaissance sorties. Early in February he received a request to take low-level oblique photographs of an airfield on the Chinese mainland.

I was reluctant to use the Spitfire PR 19 for the job, because they were painted blue and would be easily seen from above. However, No. 28 Squadron at the nearby airfield of Sek Kong was in the process of converting from Spitfire FR 18s to Vampires. I was able to acquire one of the camouflaged FR 18s and, with an oblique camera fitted in the rear fuselage, I flew the sortie. Afterwards I retained that aircraft as my personal machine for low altitude photography.

By mid-May Powles had flown sixteen flights to photograph targets in China, for the most part in coastal areas within a hundred miles of Kai Tak. He then received a request to photograph a rather more difficult target, the dock area and airfield at Yulin on the island of Hainan. Powles could have refused the job, but he regarded it as a challenge. It turned out to be the most memorable of the clandestine missions he undertook.

Flight Lieutenant Ted Powles flew numerous clandestine reconnaissance missions to photograph targets in China during 1951 and 1952. (*Powles*)

When Powles started to plan the flight in detail, he found the distance to be covered was close to the radius of action of the Spitfire PR 19. After take off from Kai Tak he would head south-east for 50 nm, climbing to 30,000 feet. He would turn southwest and head for a point 50 nm to the south-east of Yulin. From there he would head west-northwest for 40 nm, then fly due north until he reached the coast of Hainan. After identifying his position, he planned to make his first photographic run flying east-to-west through the target area. He calculated that he could just cover the required area by making two photographic runs at 30,000 feet. That was well below the altitude capability of the Mark 19, but photographs taken from higher altitudes would have too large a scale to show the amount of ground detail the photo interpreters needed. On completion of the return west-to-east run he would turn south, and return to Kai Tak using the same route as on the outbound flight. If the sortie went according to plan, the Spitfire would return to Kai Tak with about 20 minutes worth of fuel left in her tanks.

Having received favourable weather reports from Tourane in French Indo-China, Powles planned to take off at 10.00 hours on 22 May. He was in his office before 08.00 hours to make a thorough check of the Spitfire and her cameras.

I took off on time, and as I began the climb to cruising altitude the weather looked good. I could see about two-tenths cloud to the west over China but none over the sea. Twenty-six minutes after turning on to the south-westerly course I saw clouds building up to the west. Fifteen minutes later I noticed a heavy layer of cloud at about 20,000 feet over the northern part of Hainan Island. That was not a good sign.

As I was about to turn north towards Yulin I saw a layer of cirrostratus cloud over the coast, base about 28,000 feet. My orders were not to descend below 30,000 feet, but I also had a job to do. The cloud layer was thin, the light was good and the weather was fine. I decided to fly the photographic runs at 27,000 feet, though at this altitude I would require three runs to cover the whole of the target area instead of the two I had planned.

I identified the starting point for the first run and turned on to it. Then I levelled out the aircraft and turned on the cameras, checking that the lights on the control unit were flashing in the correct sequence. Throughout the run, I kept a constant watch for approaching aircraft.

When the first run was complete, I banked the aircraft steeply to port to confirm that I had photographed the required area. As I tried to identify the starting point for the second run, I found there was a large discrepancy between my map and the area below me. So for that run I had to line up on a prominent feature about one-third of the way along my intended track. The third photo run proved even more difficult, because Yulin airfield had been enlarged and had its runways extended since the map was drawn. I decided to fly a new heading that would allow the cameras to take in as much of the airfield as possible.

As he neared the end of his third run, Powles saw the sun glint off a couple of aircraft approaching him from the north. They were at about 20,000 feet and he could not tell their type. He completed the photo run then, as a precaution, he climbed into the layer of cloud and headed south over the sea. He emerged from cloud a few minutes later, to find clear skies with no sign of the other aircraft. He then climbed to 36,000 feet, levelled off and throttled back to get the optimum cruise settings for this variant of the Spitfire.

PS852, the Spitfire PR 19 that Ted Powles flew during his first clandestine reconnaissance sortie to photograph targets in China.

That unplanned third photographic run over the target area had bitten deeply into the Spitfire's fuel reserve. Even if he flew the direct route to Kai Tak, Powles calculated that he would arrive with only about five minutes worth of fuel remaining. He therefore reduced altitude slowly to 22,000 feet, the Mark 19's optimum altitude when flying for maximum range.

As an old flying adage assures us, when a pilot starts to run short of fuel the problem rarely comes alone. About thirty minutes after leaving the target, Powles entered the bank of cloud he had seen on my way out. Inside the cloud it was raining, and soon the aircraft started to get nose-heavy. As the super-cooled water droplets struck the aircraft, they were forming ice along the wing leading edge. In other circumstances Powles would have increased power to climb above

the hazard, but he did not have enough fuel for that. So he descended below the cloud and levelled out at 15,000 feet. There was no further build-up of ice, and within a few minutes the ice on the wings had melted or fallen off.

Once within VHF range of Hong Kong approach control, Powles called for a course to steer and the latest met information at Kai Tak. The airfield had six-tenths cloud, base 1,800 feet. When fifteen minutes from Kai Tak, Powles eased back on the throttle to commence a slow descent from 15,000 feet.

As I passed through 7,000 feet I was able to ascertain my position relative to the airfield and continued the descent at 1,000 feet per minute. With less than 5 gallons of fuel I called Kai Tak tower and asked for an emergency landing on Runway 31.

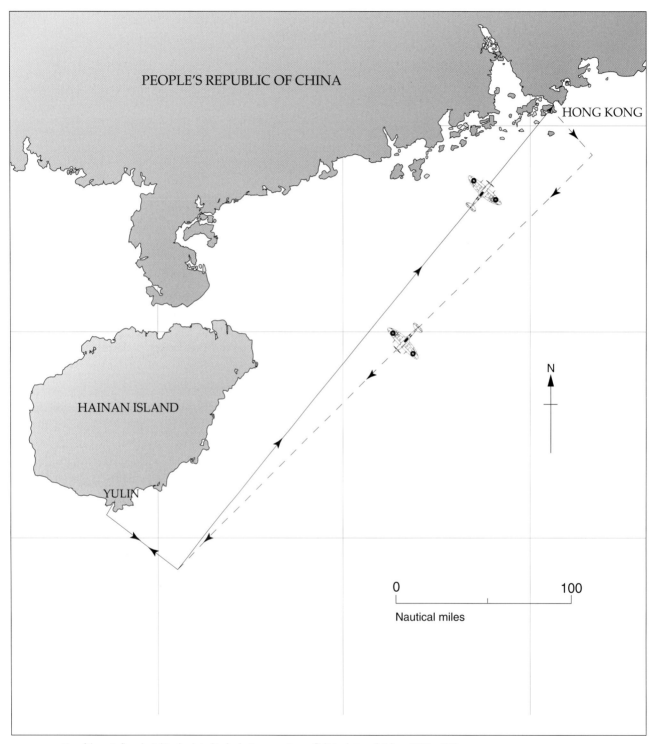

PEOPLE'S REPUBLIC OF CHINA

HONG KONG

HAINAN ISLAND

YULIN

N

0   100

Nautical miles

Map of the route flown by Ted Powles during his clandestine reconnaissance flight to photograph Yulin on 22 May 1951.

Spitfire PR 19s lined up after overhaul at South Marston, awaiting delivery to the Royal Swedish Air Force. In 1948 that service purchased fifty examples of this variant, where it was designated the S 31 and served with the reconnaissance unit Flottilj 11. The type remained in service with the RSAF until 1955.

The controller came back with a negative reply – on that runway there was a tail wind gusting between 12 to 17 knots. He did however clear me to land on Runway 07, a little-used short strip with hills at the far end, on which overshoots were forbidden.

I maintained 1,700 feet until I was over Kowloon Bay, then started my landing approach. By then the needle of the fuel gauge was bouncing on the empty mark. As I turned on to the runway heading I lowered the undercarriage. As I was about to lower the flaps, the engine suddenly stopped. I was out of fuel. The wheels touched down on the grass just short of the runway, the aircraft bounced once and then we were on the runway. The time was

1330 hours, I had been airborne for three and a half hours.

The photographs Powles had taken of Yulin were well received, and afterwards he received official thanks for a job well done.

Powles continued flying reconnaissance sorties throughout the rest of the year and much of 1952, and by the end of his two-year tour at Hong Kong he had completed 104 of these missions. Surprisingly, it appeared there was never any serious attempt to intercept the Spitfire. From time to time Powles had seen aircraft or condensation trails some distance away and coming towards him, but on each occasion a high-speed dash out to sea had been sufficient to throw off any intending pursuer.

CHAPTER 17

THE SPITFIRE:
SIGNIFICANT DATES AND SUPERLATIVES

The prototype Spitfire, K5054, made her first flight on 5 March 1936. The career of this noteworthy aircraft is described in Chapter 1.

The first production Spitfire, K9787, made her first flight in May 1938. After serving for more than two years in a trials capacity, this aircraft was converted into a PR IC and served with the Photographic Reconnaissance Unit. She failed to return from a mission in June 1941.

The first Spitfire delivered to a front-line RAF unit was the third production aircraft, K9789, which arrived at No. 19 Squadron at Duxford on 4 August 1938. This aircraft later served with No. 65 Squadron, before she was converted to the photographic reconnaissance role in July 1940 and served with the Photographic Reconnaissance Unit. Early the following month the aircraft suffered damage in a flying accident. After repair, she spent the rest of her flying career at operational training units before going to a technical training school late in 1944.

The first Spitfire to be exported was the 251st production aircraft, delivered to the French Air Force in July 1939. Evaluated at that service's test centre at Orleans/Bricy, she was still there in June 1940 when German troops overran the area.

When Great Britain declared war on Germany on 3 September 1939, the RAF had taken delivery of 306 Spitfires. Of these, 187 served with Nos 19, 41, 54, 65, 66, 72, 74, 602, 603, 609 and 611 Squadrons. Of the remainder, 71 were held at maintenance units ready for issue, 11 were serving as trials machines at the makers or the various service test establishments, 1 was allocated to the Central Flying School for the preparation of Pilots' Notes, and the remaining 36 had been written off in accidents.

Spitfires first fired their guns in anger on 6 September 1939, during the so-called 'Battle of Barking Creek'. That day a fault at the Chain Home radar station at Canewdon in Essex caused aircraft airborne to the *west* of the station to appear on the screen as if they were to the *east* of the radar (i.e. the direction from which a German attack was expected). Several fighter units were scrambled to intercept the 'intruders', and as more fighters took off the phantom 'raiding force' appeared to grow in size. In the chaos that ensued, Spitfires of No. 74 Squadron 'bounced' Hurricanes of No. 56 Squadron and shot down two of them. Following the incident, the provision of IFF radar identification equipment became a top priority requirement for RAF fighters.

Spitfires first encountered hostile aircraft on 16 October 1939, when Nos 602 and 603 Squadrons engaged nine Junkers 88A-1 bombers of *Kampfgeschwader 30* attacking Royal Navy warships in the Firth of Forth.

The first Spitfire exported was the 251st production aircraft, delivered to the French Air Force in July 1939. Evaluated at the test centre at Orleans/Bricy, she was captured when German troops overran the area in June 1940. (*Gentilli*)

Flight Lieutenant Pat Gifford of No. 603 Squadron shot down one bomber and Flight Lieutenants G. Pinkerton and A. McKellar of No. 602 Squadron shared in the destruction of another. A further Ju 88 suffered damage.

The first operational reconnaissance sortie by a Spitfire took place on 18 November 1939, as described in Chapter 6.

The first action involving a cannon-armed Spitfire was on 13 January 1940. L1007, carrying the prototype installation with two French-built Hispano 20 mm cannon, engaged a Heinkel 111 off the coast of Scotland and inflicted damage. Conventionally armed Spitfires of No. 602 Squadron then finished off the bomber.

The first Spitfires to deploy to a base outside Great Britain belonged to No. 212 Squadron, a photographic reconnaissance unit which maintained a detachment at Seclin in France from February until June 1940. The unit's work is described in Chapter 6.

Spitfire fighters saw action over Northern Europe for the first time on 12 May 1940, two days after opening of the German campaign against France, Belgium and Holland. Six Spitfires of No. 66 Squadron, in company with six Defiants, flew on an offensive over the Dutch coast and inflicted damage on a Junkers 88 bomber.

On 1 July 1940, when the Battle of Britain opened, nineteen out of the fifty single-seat fighter squadrons in RAF Fighter Command

A Spitfire Mark I, L1007, carried the prototype installation of the 20 mm Hispano cannon fitted with two French-built weapons. This aircraft first saw action on 13 January 1940.

operated Spitfires. These units had on strength a total of 292 Spitfires, of which 199 (68 per cent) were serviceable.

Probably the Spitfire with the shortest service life was X4110. Delivered as a replacement to No. 602 Squadron at Westhampnett on the morning of 18 August 1940, she was flown in action by Flight Lieutenant Dunlop Urie a couple of hours later and suffered severe damage in combat with Bf 109s. Urie landed the aircraft, but her back was broken and she never flew again.

The top scoring Fighter Command unit during the Battle of Britain was No. 603 Squadron, operating Spitfires. It moved to Hornchurch at the end of August, and from

then on it was in action almost continually. Its ranks included a number of highly effective pilots including its commander, George Denholm, Flying Officer Brian Carbury and Pilot Officer 'Razz' Berry. Recent research indicates that the unit scored 57 victories during the Battle. The second ranking unit during the Battle, No. 609 Squadron, which also operated Spitfires, scored 48 victories.

How did the Spitfire compare with the Hurricane during the Battle of Britain? Recent research shows that in any particular action, Spitfires and Hurricanes achieved victories in proportion to the number of each type taking part. Thus, as destroyers of enemy planes, the two types appear to have been about equal.

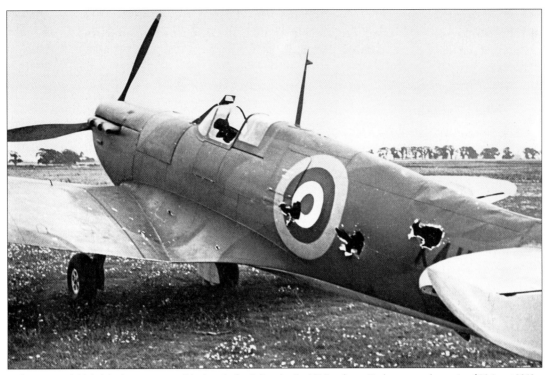

Spitfire X4110 probably had the shortest operational life of any Spitfire. Delivered to No. 602 Squadron at Westhampnett on the morning of 18 August 1940, Flight Lieutenant Dunlop Urie took her into action a couple of hours later even before there was time to paint the squadron identification letters on the fuselage. The Spitfire suffered severe damage in combat with Bf 109s and although Urie landed her successfully, her back was broken and she was written off. (*Urie*)

The Hurricane was the more ruggedly built of the two fighters, and it was the easier to repair if it suffered battle damage. Against that, the Hurricane's fuel system was the more vulnerable of the two, with an unprotected fuel tank in each wing root. If a fuel tank was hit and set ablaze, the fighter's fate was sealed. Moreover the Spitfire's superior performance, and in particular its better rate of climb, meant that it was less likely to be 'bounced' by enemy fighters attacking from above.

During major actions in the Battle, Spitfires suffered loss rates of around 4 per cent of those committed. In the case of Hurricanes, the loss rates were around 6 per cent of those committed. Because the Spitfire squadrons suffered significantly lower average attrition, they could spend longer in action. On average, Spitfire units spent 19.9 days in action during the Battle, compared with 15.6 days for the fully-engaged Hurricane squadrons (that analysis excludes the four Hurricane squadrons that remained outside the Battle area and played little part in the fighting). Recent research credits the nineteen Spitfire squadrons with 521 victories, an average of just over 27 per squadron. The thirty fully engaged Hurricane squadrons are credited with 655 victories, an average of just under 22 per squadron. During the Battle the average victory-to-loss ratio for Spitfire units was 1.8, compared with 1.34 for the fully engaged Hurricane units.

The top scoring pilot flying Spitfires during the Battle of Britain (1 July to 31 October 1940) was Pilot Officer Colin Gray of No. 54 Squadron. He was credited with 15 victories, and a share in 3 more.

Perhaps the longest distance flown during an operational mission by a Spitfire was by a PR ID piloted by Flight Lieutenant David Salway on 23 September 1941. He flew from Benson to Danzig (now Gdansk in Poland) to photograph the new German battleship *Tirpitz*, and returned. In the course of that seven-hour mission, he covered a distance of about 1,500 miles.

The first deployment of a Spitfire fighter squadron to an overseas base was on 7 March 1942, when Squadron Leader Stanley Grant took off from the aircraft carrier HMS *Eagle* and led fifteen Mark Vs to Takali, Malta where they were assigned to No. 249 Squadron. This was also the first occasion on which Spitfires flew an operational mission carrying the new 90-gallon drop tanks (see Chapter 7).

One of the fastest scoring Spitfire pilots was Sgt George 'Screwball' Beurling of No. 249 Squadron. Flying Spitfire Vs in the defence of Malta during the hectic air battles of July 1942, he was credited with 15 enemy aircraft destroyed and 6 damaged during that single month. At the end of the war his victory score stood at 31, 1 shared destroyed, and 9 damaged.

The first Spitfire fighter-bomber missions took place in August 1942. No. 126 Squadron, operating the Mark Vs from Luqa, Malta, fitted its Spitfires with a rack under each wing to carry a 250-lb bomb. The squadron used these weapons during attacks on targets in Sicily.

The largest number of Spitfires lost in a single day was on 19 August 1942, during the operations in support of the landings at Dieppe. Sixty-two Spitfires were lost, out of 100 Allied aircraft lost in total.

The highest altitude engagement involving a Spitfire, and almost certainly the highest aerial combat during the Second World War, took

Flight Lieutenant David Salway carried out one of the longer operational reconnaissance missions in a Spitfire, perhaps indeed the longest, on 23 September 1941, when he flew from Benson to Danzig (now Gdansk in Poland) and returned. During the 7-hour flight his PR ID covered a distance of about 1,500 miles.

No. 126 Squadron, operating Mark Vs from Luqa, Malta, was the first unit to operate Spitfires in the fighter-bomber role. In August 1942 the squadron fitted its Spitfires with a rack under each wing to carry one 250-lb bomb, for attacks on targets in Sicily.

place on 12 September 1942. Pilot Officer Emanuel Galitzine of the Special Service Flight at Northolt was scrambled in a specially modified Spitfire IX, BF 273, to intercept a Junkers Ju 86R bomber approaching the south coast of England. He engaged the bomber at 44,000 feet, but after a short burst his port cannon jammed. Galitzine tried to deliver further attacks, but each time he did so only his starboard cannon would fire and the Spitfire yawed and lost height. The Ju 86R escaped and landed at Caen with damage to the port wing.

The longest non-stop flights made by Spitfire fighters were the ferry flights from Gibraltar to Malta – a distance of 1,380 miles or about as far as from London to St Petersburg in Russia. As described in Chapter 7 the first such flight, Operation Train, was made on 25 October 1943 and took five and a quarter hours.

The most successful Spitfire, in terms of enemy aircraft shot down, was probably Mark IX EN398, the personal aircraft of Wing Commander 'Johnnie' Johnson who commanded the Canadian Wing based at

The Junkers Ju 86R ultra high altitude bomber, one of which was intercepted over Southampton at 44,000 feet by a modified Spitfire IX flown by Pilot Officer Emanuel Galitzine of the Special Service Flight based at Northolt, on 12 September 1942. The Ju 86R suffered damage during the encounter, and the type made no further attacks on Britain. Almost certainly, that was the highest aerial combat during the Second World War.

BF273, the modified Spitfire IX which Galitzine flew during his high altitude interception.

Kenley during the spring and summer of 1943. The career of this aircraft is described in Chapter 10.

The Spitfire that saw the longest front-line wartime service was probably X4272, which first flew as a Mark I in August 1940. Soon after delivery to No. 6 Maintenance Unit in September 1940, she was modified to Mark IB standard, with an armament of two 20 mm cannon and four machine guns. She flew in action in that configuration with No. 92 Squadron. Early in 1941 she went to Rolls-Royce Ltd for conversion to Mark VB standard, fitted with a Merlin 45 engine, and returned to No. 92 Squadron. She later served for a time with No. 222 Squadron, before going into storage for just over a year. She was then selected for conversion to LF Mark VB standard, fitted with a Merlin engine with a cropped supercharger impeller optimised for low altitude operations. After modification she was issued to No. 501 Squadron at Hawkinge in October 1943, and during the next eight months she flew numerous operational sorties. On D-Day, 6 June 1944, she flew two combat patrols over Normandy. She continued to fly operations until July 1944, but thereafter her fate is uncertain.

The first German jet aircraft to be engaged by Spitfires was the V.1 flying bomb. The attack on London using these weapons began on 13 June 1944. Although Spitfire IXs and XIIs achieved a few kills, the Spitfire XIV (equipping Nos 91, 322 and 610 Squadrons) was by far the most effective variant. The first Spitfire victory was on 16 June, when Flight Lieutenant H. Moffett of No. 91 Squadron shot down a V.1 after a chase lasting about 20 miles. The most successful Spitfire pilot against the V.1s was Lieutenant Burgwal of No. 322 (Dutch) Squadron, credited with the destruction of 21 missiles including five in a single day (8 July).

The first shoot-down of a manned German jet aircraft by Spitfires was on 5 October 1944, when a dozen Mark IXs of No. 401 (Canadian) Squadron encountered a Messerschmitt 262 fighter-bomber of *Kampfgeschwader 51* at low altitude near Nijmegen in Holland. Exploiting their altitude advantage, the Spitfire pilots dived after the German jet and were able to gain sufficient speed to get within range and shoot it down.

Probably the most successful single action by a Spitfire pilot was on 29 December 1944. Flight Lieutenant 'Dick' Audet of No. 411 (Canadian) Squadron achieved his first aerial victory that day, and followed it with four more in rapid succession. His achievement in shooting down three Fw 190s and two Bf 109s was witnessed by other pilots in his squadron, and confirmed by film from his combat camera. The German fighter units involved in the engagement, *Jagdgeschwader 6, 27* and *54*, all suffered losses that day. There is evidence that the three Fw 190s Audet claimed belonged to *9th Staffel* of *JG 54*.

The top scoring Spitfire pilot was James Edgar 'Johnnie' Johnson, who ended the war with the rank of Group Captain. His first confirmed victory was on 26 June 1941, when he shot down a Bf 109 over northern France on 26 June 1941 while flying a Spitfire II with No. 616 Squadron. In June 1942, he was promoted to squadron leader and he took command of No. 610 Squadron with Spitfire Vs. His score then stood at seven enemy aircraft destroyed and one shared destroyed. In March 1943 he was promoted to wing commander and took charge of the Canadian-manned Kenley Wing equipped with Mark IXs and Mark Vs. During the next six months he added 14 victories to his total and shared in the destruction of six more. In March 1944, following a rest tour, he returned to the front line and was appointed commander of the Canadian-manned No. 144 Wing with Mark IXs. He led this unit during the Normandy invasion and during the months that followed. In August, the Wing was disbanded and he took command of No. 127 Wing until early in 1945. On 6 April 1945 he was promoted Group Captain and appointed commander of No. 127 Wing equipped with Mark XIVs, but between then and the end of the conflict he did not add to his score.

'Johnnie' Johnson's total victory score was 34 enemy aircraft destroyed, 7 shared destroyed, 3 and 2 shared probably destroyed, 10 and 3 shared damaged and 1 shared destroyed on the ground. He achieved all his victories while flying Spitfires.

The role executed by the Spitfire that was probably furthest from its designer's mind was that of anti-submarine aircraft. During April 1945 No. 91 Squadron, the first unit to receive Spitfire 21s, began operations with the new variant flying from Ludham in Norfolk. The unit flew armed reconnaissance missions over Holland, keeping a special watch for German one-man midget submarines which at that time were active off the coast. On the morning of 26 April Flight Lieutenants W. Marshall and J. Draper caught one of these craft on the surface near the shore and strafed it with cannon. The boat was seen to sink, leaving wreckage and a large patch of oil on the surface.

During the Second World War the largest foreign user of Spitfires was the Soviet Air Force, which received a total of 1330 Spitfires Marks V and IX during the war.

The next largest foreign user of Spitfires was the US Army Air Force, which received 872 of these aircraft under reverse Lend-Lease and used them extensively over Northern Europe, North Africa and Italy. As well as the aircraft delivered to front-line units, that service also received at least one example of almost every production version of the Spitfire for test and evaluation.

The longest distance flight ever made by a Spitfire was by Captain James Storey, in a PR XI, on 3 May 1947. The Spitfire covered the 1,850 miles from Dakar in Senegal to Natal in Brazil in just over eight hours, as related in Chapter 14.

The final Spitfire built, Mark 24 VN496, came off the Supermarine production line at South Marston on 24 February 1948. After a period of storage at the RAF Maintenance Unit at Brize Norton, she was issued to No. 80 Squadron and went with the unit to Hong Kong in August 1949. She was written off in an accident in December 1950.

The last Spitfire fighter unit in RAF regular service was No. 80 Squadron based at Kai Tak, Hong Kong. This unit was also the only regular RAF unit to operate the Spitfire F.24, from January 1948 to January 1952.

The last RAF Spitfire flights to venture over hostile territory were the clandestine operations to photograph targets in the People's Republic of China during 1951 and 1952. These missions, flown by PR 19s of No. 81 Squadron from Kai Tak, Hong Kong, are described in Chapter 16.

The last operational sortie by an RAF Spitfire took place on 1 April 1954 when a PR 19 of No. 81 Squadron, PS888 based at Seletar, Singapore, flew a photographic mission over an area of jungle in Johore thought to contain Communist guerrillas.

The Soviet Air Force was the largest foreign operator of Spitfires. In 1943 that service received 143 Mark Vs, one of which is depicted here fitted with a radio homing loop aerial. Later that service also received 1,185 Spitfire IXs. (*via Guest*)

The Soviet Air Force converted a few Spitfire IXs into two-seat trainers. (*via Guest*)

A Spitfire F.24 of No. 80 Squadron based at Kai Tak, Hong Kong. This was the last regular unit in the RAF to operate a fighter version of the Spitfire, and it gave up the last of these aircraft in January 1952. (*Powles*)

Probably the final offensive missions flown by Spitfires were those by the Burmese (now the Union of Myanmar) Air Force during 1955 and 1956, operating against insurgent bands in rural areas. In 1948, the BAF received three Spitfirc FR 18s. In 1951 it took delivery of twenty denavalised Seafire XVs, with non-folding wings and the arrester hooks removed. In 1955, the service received twenty-two Spitfire IXs purchased from Israel. The Burmese Air Force employed its Spitfires and Seafires in the fighter-bomber and reconnaissance roles.

The last flight by a Spitfire in regular RAF service was by PR 19 (PS853) in June 1957, when civilian pilot John Formby (a retired Flight Lieutenant) of the THUM (Temperature and Humidity) Flight operating from Woodvale in Lancashire took off for a meteorological observation sortie.

The last warlike act performed by an RAF Spitfire was by a PR 19. In 1963, the Indonesian government was engaged in a military confrontation aimed at seizing part of what is now Malaysia. If it came to an armed conflict, the RAF needed to know how its Mach 2 Lightning fighters could best deal with the P-51 Mustang fighters operated by the Indonesian Air Force. Accordingly, a battle trial was laid on pitting a Lightning against a Spitfire PR 19, PM631, which had broadly similar performance characteristics to the Mustang. Provided the Lightning did not drop its speed and allow itself to be drawn into a close combat turning fight with its more agile opponent, the Spitfire (or

171

PR.19 PS888 flew the last operational sortie by an RAF Spitfire, on 1 April 1954. Taking off from Seletar, Singapore, she photographed an area in Johore thought to contain hideouts for Communist guerrillas. For the occasion the Spitfire's nose carried the appropriate inscription, 'The Last!' (*Peck*)

In 1951 the Burmese (now the Union of Myanmar) Air Force took delivery of twenty denavalised Seafire XVs, fitted with non-folding Spitfire F.18 wings and with the arrester hook and other items of naval equipment removed. Midway between a Spitfire and a Seafire, this interesting hybrid took part in what were probably the final offensive missions by either type, operating in the fighter-bomber and reconnaissance roles against insurgents in 1955 and 1956.

PS 915 was one of three Spitfire PR 19s operated by the Meteorological Flight based at Woodvale, Lancashire. The Flight conducted regular weather observations and measurements until it was disbanded in June 1957, to end the Spitfire's service in the regular RAF.

Mustang) stood little chance in such an encounter. The Lightning's most effective tactic was to position itself several thousand feet below its opponent in the latter's blind zone, and attack it in a steep climb using its Firestreak infra-red homing missiles.

The oldest surviving Spitfire is K9942, a Mark I delivered to No. 72 Squadron at Church Fenton on 24 April 1939. She was flown several times by Flight Officer James Nicholson who, flying Hurricanes with No. 249 Squadron during the Battle of Britain, gained the only Victoria Cross awarded to a fighter pilot. K9942 was damaged in a landing accident on 4 June 1940, and following repairs she went to No. 57 Operational Training Unit at Hawarden. The aircraft is currently on display at the RAF Museum at Hendon.

The oldest surviving airworthy Spitfire at the time of writing is P7350, a Mark II. She made her first flight at Castle Bromwich in August 1940 and was delivered to No. 266 (Rhodesia) Squadron at Wittering on 6 September. In the months to follow she served with Nos 64, 603 and 616 Squadrons. In August 1941, after an overhaul, she went into storage for a time. In April 1942 she was issued to the Central Gunnery School at Sutton Bridge, where in February 1943 she suffered damage in an accident. After repair she went to No. 57 Operational Training Unit where in April 1944 she again suffered damage in an accident. After repair she went to No. 39 Maintenance Unit at Colerne and spent the rest of the war in storage. Currently she flies with the RAF Battle of Britain Memorial Flight based at Conningsby, Lincolnshire.

Spitfire 21s undergoing final
assembly at the South
Marston factory, in 1945.

A Spitfire F.22 in company with a pre-production Supermarine Swift fighter in 1951. Despite its illustrious ancestry, the Swift was not a success in the fighter role and after a brief service career the type was withdrawn from service. (*RAF Museum, Charles Brown*)

SPECIFICATIONS OF MAJOR SPITFIRE VARIANTS

For a full account of the development of the Spitfire, and detailed performance figures on each of the various versions, see *The Spitfire Story* by Alfred Price, Arms and Armour Press.

	Mark I[1]	Mark V[2]	Mark IX[3]	Mark XII[4]	Mark XIV[5]	Mark 21[6]
Span	36 ft 10 in	36 ft 10 in	36 ft 10 in	36 ft 10 in	36 ft 10 in	40 ft 4 in
Length	29 ft 11 in	29 ft 11 in	30 ft 0 in	30 ft 9 in	32 ft 8 in	32 ft 8 in
Maximum take-off weight	5819 lb	6525 lb	7400 lb	7415 lb	8400 lb	9124 lb
Power	Merlin II 1030 hp	Merlin 45 1470 hp	Merlin 61 1560 hp	Griffon IIB 1700 hp	Griffon 61 2035 hp	Griffon 61 2035 hp
Maximum speed	362 mph	371 mph	409 mph	397 mph	446 mph	457 mph
Service ceiling	31,900 ft	37,500 ft	38,000 ft	32,800 ft	44,000 ft	43,000 ft
Gun armament	8 × .303 in	2 × 20 mm 4 × .303 in	2 × 20 mm 4 × .303 in	2 × 20 mm 4 × .303 in	2 × 20 mm 4 × .303 in	4 × 20 mm

1. These data refer to the first production Spitfire, K9787, during trials in May 1938.
2. These data refer to an early production aircraft, W3134, during trials in May 1941.
3. These data refer to the development aircraft AB505, during trials in April 1942.
4. These data refer to the prototype Mark XII, DP845, during trials in September 1942 when she was fitted with a standard-span wing. Production Mark XIIs had clipped wings, span 32ft 8in.
5. These data refer to the development aircraft JF319, during trials in September 1943.
6. These data refer to the prototype Mark 21, PP139, during trials late in 1943 when she was fitted with extended-span pointed wings. Production Mark 21s were fitted with rounded wing tips, span 36 ft 11 in.

BIBLIOGRAPHY

Aeroplane Spotter magazine, series on the Spitfire, June 1946 to October 1947

Cross, Roy and Scarborough, Gerald, *Spitfire*, Patrick Stephens

Harvey-Bayley, Alec, *The Merlin in Perspective*, Rolls-Royce Heritage Trust

Hooton, Ted, *Spitfire Special*, Ian Allan

——, *Supermarine Spitfire Mk I–XVI*, Osprey

——, *Supermarine Spitfire Mk XII–24*, Osprey

Morgan, Eric and Shacklady, Edward, *Spitfire, the History*, Key Publishing

Moss, Peter, *Spitfire*, Ducimus

Price, Alfred, *Battle of Britain Day*, Greenhill Books

——, *Battle of Britain, the Hardest Day*, Orion

——, *Late Marque Spitfire Aces*, Osprey

——, *Spitfire Mark I/II Aces* Osprey

——, *Spitfire Mark V Aces*, Osprey

——, *Spitfire: a Documentary History*, Janes

——, *Spitfire at War, Vols 1, 2 and 3*, Ian Allan

——, *The Spitfire Story*, Arms and Armour Press

RAF Handbook, *The Spitfire V Manual*, reprinted by Arms and Armour Press

Robertson, Bruce, *Spitfire – the Story of a Famous Fighter*, Harleyford

Various authors, *Forty Years of the Spitfire*, Royal Aeronautical Society

Taylor, John and Alward, Maurice, *Spitfire*, Harborough

INDEX